*In Loving Memory of Karen Fund
and Sandra Hopkins*

SURROGATE

How A Woman Named Sandra Made Me A Mother

By Karen L. Fund

International Psychoanalytic Books (IPBooks)
New York • http://www.IPBooks.net

Published by IPBooks, Queens, NY
Online at: www.IPBooks.net

Copyright © 2020 David James Fisher

All rights reserved. This book may not be reproduced, transmitted, or stored, in whole or in part by any means, including graphic, electronic, or mechanical without the express permission of the author and/or publisher, except in the case of brief quotations embodied in critical articles and reviews.

ISBN: 978-1-949093-57-5

To my children Benjamin and Chloe,

and to Sandra

With all the love in a mother's heart.

Contents

Preface ix

Chapter 1
    The Dalcon Shield IUD 1

Chapter 2
    On Not Getting Pregnant 7

Chapter 3
    The Medical Side of Infertility 11

Chapter 4
    Putting Reproduction Behind 25

Chapter 5
    Facing the Options 27

Chapter 6
    Choosing Surrogacy 33

Chapter 7
    Llana 37

Chapter 8
    Sandra 61

Karen L. Fund In Context
 by David James Fisher 87

A Conversation with Sandra Hopkins
 by David James Fisher 105

A Surrogate Daughter's Ambivalence
 by Chloe B. Fisher 117

Karen L. Fund Biography 121

Preface

INFERTILITY HAS REACHED almost epidemic proportions, being far more widespread than ever before. I've heard that statistically there are one in five couples in America who are infertile. Twenty percent of all marriages are suffering with the heartbreaking inability to have a child.

When I was growing up, you rarely heard of a child being adopted. The whole topic was shrouded in secrecy and shame. Few of us actually knew someone personally who was adopted. This was, in fact, because there were lesser needs for adoption; fewer women than today were having trouble getting pregnant. A woman who couldn't bear a child was singular in her experience in that way and very unique from the rest of married women.

That's just not so now. Infertility is far from uncommon. Today, you're very likely to hear about a friend or several friends, a family member, or perhaps yourself, who can't have a child. It's not at all unusual to know a person or even several people who have adopted their child. The difference between now and thirty years ago is the sharp increase in the inability of women to have children.

My own belief is that there are several reasons for this. One reason certainly is that women are having children later. In so doing, their bodies function differently in their late thirties and throughout their forties than they did in their twenties.

I think another factor is that we are now dealing with an unparalleled level of pollutants in the air and in our food. These additives, chemicals, dyes, and pollutants have a cumulative effect on the body, and I suspect these toxins have contributed to an adverse effect on the delicate balance in a woman's reproductive system.

Both these factors I suspect play a part, but I think another reason that so many women are having trouble getting pregnant is that we have stepped into roles that, until quite recently, women have never held. We have assumed these positions by our own efforts and dedication and I'm terribly glad that we were successful in doing so. However, one result has been a marked increase in the level of stress and pressure in our lives. We are rising high in business, managing our jobs, managing our families, managing our homes. Many of us are responsible as doctors and as attorneys and executives in business. Historically, women rarely held that kind of responsibility. These new roles that we have carved out for ourselves couldn't be more positive and our success in achieving this, despite the still existing double standard, has been remarkable. But I sense that in addition to all of the gains, we have also paid a price. I think we've paid many prices, but one of them has been the terrific toll that stress and responsibility has taken on our bodies' exquisite balance and harmony.

Surrogate adoption is almost summarily dismissed by most people as extremely dangerous with too much potential for heartbreak. Few people know that surrogacy has been with us and quietly working for many couples since biblical times and indeed is written of in the Bible. But one woman, Mary Beth Whitehead, managed to all but destroy what is one of the few options available to childless women. She created, in the wake of her media orgy, what has become the national point of view on surrogacy. The first thing people think of when they hear the words surrogate adoption is Mary Beth Whitehead, and a child, a baby, being ripped away from her adoptive parents when Whitehead decided to change her mind and take the baby back. That kind of devastating experience no one wants to endure, so many would never even consider surrogate adoption. In most states, surrogacy is illegal now. In all states, surrogacy is suspect. This is a terrible shame especially in light of how positive the surrogacy experience can be — as it was for me.

CHAPTER 1

The Dalcon Shield IUD

ALTHOUGH I DIDN'T KNOW it at the time, my birth control was slowly and silently sterilizing me.

It happened at age 28 with the Copper 7 Dalcon Shield IUD. I had been having problems with birth control pills. Today, birth control pills carry a much lower dosage of estrogen yet are equally as effective. But the estrogen levels in the early 1970's were much higher and the side effects for women who were sensitive to it were severe. That was the case for me. The weight gain which resulted from being on the pill wasn't just a pesky little five pounds; it was a significant amount of water weight which caused pressure and pain. My breasts swelled and became just too painful. Drastic mood changes were overwhelming and misinterpreted. My mother's sister had breast cancer and there was some talk, even in the early days, that history of cancer in the mother's family was something to be looked at closely before being prescribed birth control pills.

I talked with my physician about it. He recommended and prescribed the Copper 7 IUD. He was enthusiastic about the IUD which was then being touted as a modern miracle birth control for women. It was called a Copper 7 because it was made out of copper and it was shaped just like the number seven. My doctor assured me that it was safe and was the answer to my problems. I would no longer have to take hormones, nor would I have to remember to take a pill every day. I would not feel it and my partner would not feel it. It would be unnoticeable and invisible in my body. For as long as I would wear the IUD, I would be free of the fear of pregnancy and the side effects of large doses of hormones. I could wear it safely for years and whenever I wanted it out, it could be removed easily. That sounded good. I felt comfortable with the idea when I agreed to have the IUD put in. It was inserted into my cervix in the doctor's office. The procedure was horrifically painful, but it was brief and when it was over the pain disappeared.

    I trusted the doctor. He assured me it was safe, and I believed him. After a while, I began to have problems with the IUD. Sadly, I believed the doctors who continued to reassure me that it was safe and what I was describing was normal. The problems began with extremely heavy periods. I used to have to wear sometimes three Tampax at once with the strings tied together to make sure that one didn't go up too far. Even with that, I would often wake up and the sheets would be bloody. The cramping was severe. The doctor's response to my concerns were, "That's the thing about the IUD, you will get a heavy period. But look at the benefits of it. You don't have to worry about taking a pill, you don't have to worry about the side effects of the pill, you don't have to think about the IUD. It's there doing its job and except for temporary, heavy bleeding and cramping, it's a completely benign object."

My periods continued this way every month for as long as the IUD was in and the heavy bleeding and cramping continued to get worse. I would spend the day changing Tampax. And my periods didn't last for the typical three or four days; they were usually eight to ten days long. Again, I went to the doctor and I talked to him about it and again he said there was nothing unusual about what I was describing and that if I could live with that, I would enjoy all the benefits of the IUD. And since he told me there was nothing to worry about, I didn't worry; I just accepted it as the price I had to pay to be free of concern of an unwanted pregnancy.

But my concern came back. It was after a boyfriend of mine spent the night at my house for the first time. I remember pulling back the covers and although the sheets were laundered, they were badly stained. The stains had become so familiar to me, I almost didn't see them anymore, but he was shocked. He said, "My God, what happened here? Was there a murder that took place in your house?" I looked at him and said, "Oh, the sheets are clean, it's just that the stains remain after washing." He said, "I'm not concerned that your sheets aren't clean, I'm concerned about you. How could it be that so much blood would be on your sheets?" The fact that somebody else was so shocked at the sight finally awakened me that maybe this wasn't an acceptable situation. I went back to the doctor.

Again, I expressed my concerns. His exasperated and annoyed response was a thinly veiled message of: "If you want to fuck around and have a free sexual life, then this is the price you're going to just have to pay. If you're willing to abstain from sex, then I'll take this thing out and you won't have anything to worry about." His discourse was dripping with disapproval and patronization. Inherent in it was a schoolteacher's tone of voice towards a student who had misbehaved. That was the feeling I had when he was talking to me. Infantilizing.

Reprimanded and pulled up short, pathetically, I responded exactly the way so many of us did at the time and it was exactly what he expected. I recoiled and stuck my head back into my shell and didn't say another word about it. Keep in mind this was nearly twenty years ago. The world was a very different place then for women. Today it's unthinkable for me to imagine letting a doctor get away with being so insulting and controlling.

In 1978, I met a wonderful man named Jim, whom I eventually married. I was wearing the IUD when we first began dating in Tucson, Arizona. Jim told me that he could feel the IUD when we were making love. He said he could feel something hard touching him. I went back to the doctor again, but this time I said, "This can't be right. The one thing you've told me all along is that I won't feel the IUD and my partner won't feel it. Well, he can." The doctor conceded to taking an X-Ray. In all my prior visits, in response to all my questions and concerns, the doctor had never checked the IUD, had never taken an X-Ray.

I could see for myself, when he put my X-ray up to the light, that the IUD was not in my cervix where it was supposed to be, it was dug into the wall of my uterus and sticking through the cervix. And it was upside down. It was no longer a "7", it was an "L." The doctor said, "Well, we're going to have to take this out."

If you think the IUD was painful going in, in its proper position, coming out, upside down was indescribable. Never did the doctor suggest that he anesthetize me; he just did it. The IUD did not come out as quickly as it had gone in, so it was torture until it finally was removed.

It was only years later that I was to learn that the entire time that IUD was in my body, it was undetectably scarring the inside of my fallopian tubes to the point where nothing again would ever pass through them. Scar tissue had been building year after year after year and was now so thick an egg would never be able to move down in the normal way it was meant to and begin a pregnancy.

I became one of the thousands of women who were permanently sterilized from the Copper 7 Dalcon Shield.

CHAPTER 2

On Not Getting Pregnant

I FELL SO DEEPLY IN LOVE with Jim. I felt towards him like I had never felt towards anybody. He was the man for me. I knew, or at least I hoped, that I would marry him someday. He wasn't so sure at that point, but I was extremely determined. He moved away from Tucson and went to Los Angeles. I followed him. I had to! I moved into his apartment, practically without his permission. And about a year after we began living together, we got married. To this day, our marriage remains one of the very best things that ever happened to me. Almost immediately, we stopped using any kind of birth control and I began to psychologically prepare myself for imminent motherhood.

I, like most women of my generation, grew up with the absolute, unshakable belief that I would one day fall in love, get married, and have a baby. This was carefully socialized into us in a myriad of ways, from fairy tales that we were read, to many subtle messages sent to girls from birth to puberty. You don't really have a life until the prince kisses you, awakening you from a deep sleep, and with that kiss, brings you to life.

The socialization worked for me and I certainly always believed that I would get married and have a child. As a little girl, I would play act at being my mother. I used to pretend to be sitting at a dinner table with my make-believe husband with make-believe children. Every movie, book, fairy tale, and television commercial told me so. I had no doubt this would be my destiny. As unwavering as my faith that one day I would marry, I was just as sure that a pregnancy before marriage would ruin my life. I had always been so frightened at the prospect of getting pregnant; probably because my mother made a particular issue of that when I was growing up. I had a vivid, omnipresent, and electrifying fear of pregnancy. My mother told me that if a boy's semen comes in contact with you, even if it's on your leg (I thought that meant even through clothing), that somehow it could go up and into you and you could then get pregnant. Listen, if you don't let a boy come in contact with your leg, he's pretty much not going to get near the inside of your vagina. So, my mother had figured that out perfectly. I was sure things were exactly as my mother had described and that my life would be ruined if I ever was to be so unfortunate and wretched as to get pregnant by mistake. So, out of fear, I took particular care with birth control, often using two kinds.

So, when Jim and I were married and we retired the condoms, I assumed I would get pregnant right away. The first-time semen was finally allowed to get through, unfettered by condoms, (and clothing), I was sure I'd be pregnant within the first month. But I wasn't. Then I thought it would be the second or the third month. My dominant and most noticeable response to not getting pregnant within the first couple of months of trying was surprise. I was so sure pregnancy could and would happen if I let down my guard and was careless, even just once. I was so astonished, stunned really, that I didn't get pregnant immediately. My mother said I would, but I wasn't worried. A year went by.

I was now about thirty-five. In those days, you didn't hear very much about women not being able to get pregnant. If the subject did come up, it was in little snips of conversations here and there, but it wasn't often discussed. Now you hear about it all the time. I don't know of anybody who doesn't have someone in their life who hasn't been touched by it in some way. Almost everyone has a friend who can't get pregnant, or a cousin or a sister. Many people have seen up close what infertility has done to a loved one.

After a year of trying to get pregnant with no success, I felt it was time to see what the story was. I wasn't worried, but I went to the doctor. I didn't have any idea at the time but that visit was to become the first of scores of doctor visits in the long and what was to become a desperate effort to get pregnant.

It began with basic blood tests. Some of the things that can cause difficulty in getting pregnant, the doctors assure you, are very simple. They can be discovered early, treated, and you become pregnant soon thereafter. The doctors made a big deal about that in the beginning. They reassuringly talked a lot about a small problem being detected early on, with an easy solution, quickly followed by a pregnancy. I have yet to meet a woman who has an infertility problem that was solved early and easily. I can't say it never happened, only that I never met a couple who were fortunate in that way. One of the most difficult aspects of infertility is that the doctors are so optimistic, always having something else for you to try. Every time you go through a series of tests that they suggest will produce the answer and it fails, you're moved, as if you are on a conveyer belt, to the next series of medications or procedures they can try. This did more to inflame hope than actually to be reassuring, and hope is the name of the game. If a woman loses hope, ceases to believe she can ever become pregnant, she stops going to the doctor (and the doctor stops getting paid).

My doctors talked a lot early on about the "environment of the vagina." Perhaps I was producing something in the mucus of the vagina that could be killing the sperm. It's very common, the doctors said, and it's very easy to solve. They could prescribe a medication and I'd stop killing off my husband's sperm.

Knowing me, I figured I had that! I was a spermicidal maniac! I knew it. I was a sperm killer. So, I was sure that they would test me, that's what they would find, I would be prescribed medication and this already unpleasant experience would be over. As it turned out, my mucus was very kind to Jim's sperm. Charitable really. My vagina was a kind and a gentle vagina, and it wasn't killing his sperm.

So that wasn't the problem. They give you a lot of hope at the beginning. It's very likely that they can find something quickly and easily and fix it, they say. There has been a lot of success for a great many women, they say. I guess human nature is such that you believe that will be true for you too. You must believe it. It falls in line with the original thinking that of course, you're going to have a child. And you don't doubt that. Some little glitch seems to have occurred here; they'll find it, fix it, and then you'll get on with what you were sure your life would look like.

CHAPTER 3

The Medical Side of Infertility

———·..·———

WHEN THOSE INITIAL TREATMENTS didn't work, they began stepping up the different tests and courses of action. This phase involves the prescribing of hormones. This is some of the most crazy-making stuff on earth. Hormones have a tremendously powerful effect on the body. As more about PMS is beginning to be understood, we have become aware of the painful and sometimes unmanageable effects it has on women. Chump change compared to the emotional earthquake set off in your body due to the levels of medicines prescribed in order to set a hormonal climate that is sure to make you pregnant. I was nearly paralyzed with a sense of depression, anxiety, and a black sadness. This inexplicable despair wasn't confined to the four or five days of my monthly period; it was all month long. To make matters worse, my symptoms were not taken seriously by the physician. At that time, they were generally not taken seriously by physicians, even when you weren't trying to get pregnant. And they were not taken seriously when my body was being pumped full of these drugs.

As difficult as the emotional side of it was, that was only the beginning. My gums were puffy and bleeding. At the time, I had no idea that these symptoms were connected to the medication I was being given. Nobody had given me any warning about that. It's almost unbelievable, I know, but I can't remember even one physician giving me the slightest indication that I should expect any side effects from the hormones. The swelling in my gums continued and I went to see a dentist. He referred me to a periodontist who advised that I undergo periodontal surgery immediately. He explained that I had an early deterioration of the gums and that while it was unusual for someone my age, it was not unheard of. As I later discovered, this procedure was a miserable ordeal. The dentist put me under and cut into the entire gum above every tooth and slit away a fraction of gum. After surgery, my mouth was packed for twenty-four hours. The pain continued for days and days after the surgery. And that was only the upper part of the gums. I was scheduled to return for the same procedure on the lower part of the gums. I couldn't face it. The upper was so awful and so unexpected that I couldn't go back and do it again. I chose to live with the bleeding of the gums rather than go back and have the second part of the surgery. I had paid him for the whole thing in advance and I didn't even ask to have fifty percent of it refunded. My mouth continued to bleed.

The course of actions consisting of hormone therapy did finally come to an end. It wasn't working; I wasn't getting pregnant and they did take me off the hormones. Within weeks of going off the hormones, my gums tightened up and stopped bleeding. And again, when I talked with my doctor about my gums bleeding because of the hormones, he did, in fact, get angry and resented the fact that I was questioning him. He suggested I was overreacting and yes there might be unpleasant moments, but they should not be dwelt upon. If I wanted to get pregnant, I needed to understand and accept the occasional discomforts and the disappointments and keep my resolve. That, more or less, was the typical response to any questioning or raising of concerns on my part. I was afraid of alienating him. It seemed the doctors were my only chance of getting this baby and I felt I had to be careful not to aggravate them to the point that they wouldn't want to help me anymore. It was an ugly position being infantilized that way; it definitely was one of the worst parts of the whole medical experience.

We still didn't know what was "wrong" with me at this point. The doctors were going through all these steps hoping we would hit the right one. Interestingly, they never talked about the statistics of how many women would never get pregnant. It just wasn't discussed, and I admit my own culpability in not asserting myself more by asking that important question. I feel embarrassed and ashamed by the omission.

These were the days before the ovulation predictor tests. Seems like we're talking about the dark ages and yet it was only twenty-fve years ago. The current widespread problem of infertility has spawned so many inventions for women to use to detect when they are ovulating and even home kits for pregnancy tests.

But then, without an ovulation predictor test, the process of finding the moment when you ovulate was quite aggravating and really pretty difficult. I used a special thermometer, a basil thermometer, which only has about three degrees on it. The numbers were made larger and presumably easier to read because you were now looking for a variation in a tenth of a degree. The day that my temperature rose a tenth of a degree is the day that I was ovulating. So, I was given a chart that was broken down into tenths of a degree and I kept the chart and the thermometer by my bed. When I woke up in the morning, I wasn't allowed to sit up, certainly couldn't stand, which, of course, negated any possibility of going to the bathroom. Any movement of the body raises your body temperature a little.

I had to lie very still on my back, put the thermometer in my mouth, and leave it there for five minutes. Instead of waking up in a normal way, the very first conscious fraction of my day was restrained and controlled by this event. It's different if you only do this once or twice or three times, but it becomes more than an annoyance when you have to do it week after week, month after month, for over a year. That's over two hundred mornings of trying to find a tenth of a degree change. It's a seemingly little thing that becomes more irritating and restrictive as the months pass. This process would start about a week after my period and become a constant in my life. The not being able to sit up as one normally does in the morning became symbolic to me of how I felt pushed down and helpless. And they really weren't designed well. The charts were very difficult to read. A tenth of a percent is a tiny, tiny increment and very hard to see. Thank God I was fifteen years younger and I could see! I'd be sunk now without a powerful magnifying glass. But there I was, marking my chart and waiting for the morning the thermometer would go up a tenth of a percent. That was the day I would get into the car and go during my lunch hour to the doctor to be artificially inseminated with my husband's sperm. And the next day, I'd do it again. And the next day I'd do it again. Three days in a row to create the optimal chance of hitting it right.

My office was in a community in Los Angeles called Silver Lake. Silver Lake is a good forty to forty-five-minute drive to Beverly Hills where my doctor's office was. I had to be at the doctor's office for insemination three times a month. I could not cut into my work time too much and always go during my lunch hour. But this trip to the doctor's office, start to finish, was usually two and half to three hours. While I loved my job at that time, I was Associate Publisher at *The LA Weekly*, a large weekly newspaper, it was also highly stressful. At any given time, there were at least two or three things always going on simultaneously. I was working long hours, managing a lot of responsibility, and under the pressures of weekly deadlines.

I remember coming back from the doctor's office having been gone for three hours and there would be about twenty telephone messages waiting for me to which I had to respond. To be absent from my office like this, three times a month, month after month after month for over a year became a very stressful problem in and of itself. As stressful in some ways as the infertility itself. I was lucky, though. I was working with people who cared for me and who wanted to help in any way they could. I was highly conscious of the fact that I was missing a lot of work and that I wasn't there to do what I was supposed to do during these long periods of time. I'm an anxious person by nature; I always feel under the gun and that I'm not doing enough, whether I am or not. So, I'd leave the office in a highly stressed out state to begin with and then have to get into the car (this was pre car phone) and have this dead time where I couldn't accomplish anything. I couldn't answer phone calls, I couldn't make phone calls, I couldn't do my job and now it was a forty minute drive and I'd get into the doctor's office and without exception, I would always have to wait a half hour or forty five minutes to see the doctor. I never didn't have to wait. And in the waiting room were all of these other women. I'd look around at them and they all looked a lot like I did. They looked harried, they looked defeated, and they looked desperate.

One day, a pregnant woman (the only one I ever saw there) came into the waiting room — very pregnant. It was like an electrical charge went through that waiting room; the reaction that we had to this woman in our presence was intense; she embodied everything that we ached for; everything that we were sacrificing for. I can't remember any other situation where there was such mass envy and resentment. I guess I'm what you'd call a woman's woman. I really enjoy and like women. I love to see them succeed and reach whatever are their personal goals. I almost never feel envious of other women's accomplishments. But that woman... I could have killed her. And I think that everybody else in the waiting room felt the same way. That she could come in there with all of her health and all of her normalcy. I felt ashamed of my embittered reaction, yet it was devastating to see her blossom with a growing child inside of her, when I felt so malformed and barren. I was coming to the point where it was painfully difficult to be around children or even our good friends who had children.

I am waiting in the waiting room. And I wait. I wait for forty- five minutes. Now I've been gone from the office well over and hour and a half and haven't even seen the doctor yet. I'm hungry; I haven't eaten. Then I'm called into the examination room and I take all my clothes off and I get on a gurney with only a sheet of paper with which to cover myself and then I wait again. And I wait as long as thirty minutes only to be seen by a nurse who comes in and does a quick blood pressure check and then she's gone and I'm alone again. At this point you could have baked potatoes in the heat being generated in my stomach. I am anxious and enraged and I'm desperately trying to stuff the rage down because I know how risky it is to express it to the doctor. Finally, the doctor came in and inseminated me. It took less than three minutes.

Earlier in the day, Jim had gone to my doctor's office and deposited his sperm. They do something called a "wash" which takes out any impurities in the sperm that might be there. These things are not harmful under normal intercourse situations, but if removed will make it just that much more possible for the procedure to be successful. Jim's sperm is then pulled up into a syringe and injected high into the vagina, close to the cervix (painless). After the injection, I have to lie there for another fifteen minutes because I'm told if I stand up, the sperm drips right down to the bottom of the vagina. If you lie on your back, the sperm will stay near the opening of the cervix longer and will have a better chance of getting where you want it to go. Then I get dressed and I go back to the office. A lot of time has passed. Throughout the whole process, opposite sides of the same emotional coin are operating simultaneously. On the one hand, I am sick with rage and fury that I've been kept waiting for so long and weak with relief and gratitude that the procedure's been done.

I rarely saw the doctor after the inseminations. I would just wait for the required fifteen minutes, step carefully off the table, and go back to the office. But once in a while, the doctor would invite you into his office after the procedure to have a chat with him. One day, I broached the subject of the long waiting time.

"I am mindful of the fact that as an OB-GYN, you deliver babies and you can unexpectedly be called at any time for a delivery. It's understood that you would not be able to keep an appointment if you are called to deliver a baby. But you are never here at the appointed hour. I always have to wait a half hour or forty-five minutes to see you. As a working woman, it's very hard for me to leave my office in the first place and to wait all that time before being seen." His response was one of those moments which has stayed vivid in my memory. He said, "Well, it sounds like your work is very important to you and maybe if your job is so important to you, you should really re-think whether you want to be a mother or not." He was also suggesting that maybe I wasn't worth his time. If I didn't want to be a mother badly enough to put up with whatever I had to put up with, maybe he should use that time to deal with another woman who wanted it more.

It was a remark which I can't believe today, but at the time rendered me silent.

To this day, I sometimes still find myself replaying the exchange in my head and this time, answering him.

As I left the doctor's office, I would always step gingerly, thinking that there had been a connection. Thinking that one of the sperm had found the egg and a life was starting to grow inside of me. I would leave the doctor's office feeling like a holy person.

After every insemination I would be lost in a dream. I would dream about Jim and I having a family and being parents. I would see us holding and loving our child, beginning anew. It certainly wasn't unreasonable to hope that this insemination was the one that worked.

It was a long two weeks to go through to get to the end of the month and wait. I can't describe to you how long those two weeks would take to pass. Everyday thinking this might be it. Everyday going to work, getting dressed, brushing my teeth, thinking I might have a baby inside of me. It was almost like carrying around a secret. I was very careful about my diet. I remember once going to the dentist and then being horrified, waking up in the middle of the night realizing that he had given me nitrous oxide and it may have hurt the baby. I called the dentist the next day and said, "I have to ask you this. I'm very concerned and very worried. If I'm pregnant, would the gas have hurt my child?" He said, "You weren't under very long but how far along are you?" I said, "I don't know if I'm pregnant or not." And he said, "Well how far along could you be?" And I said, "I think about 48 hours." He laughed and said, "I don't think so!" and got me off the phone as quickly as he could. For the next two weeks, I stayed aware, concerned, excited, protective, and full of hope.

Two weeks would go by and then it would get close to the day in my cycle where if I was pregnant, I would miss my period. Even when I felt the cramps and the lower back pain and my breasts beginning to swell, I would often try to interpret these menstrual symptoms to mean, instead, signs of pregnancy. But my period would come. My period came every month. The numbing disappointment is hard to explain. It felt like being dropped out of a plane. Sinking. And mustering up the energy and enthusiasm to try again was difficult. It was a morbid two week wait before I could even try it again. Waiting to ovulate, waiting to begin reading that stupid chart, waiting to take the thermometer readings, waiting and hoping that this month will be it. Sometimes my period would be late. One day late, two days late, three days late. Those months were particularly excruciating. Hope would soar. I could barely breathe no less concentrate on work. This was it! Maybe. Please, God, let this be it. But each time, my own blood, like a talisman, brought the news of another failure.

The odds were that I should be getting pregnant. There was no reason, that I had been made aware of, for not getting pregnant. I started to think of my situation and staying with my doctor like a slot machine. If you stand at a slot machine and continue to put quarters in it for an entire day, it's very hard to give up and walk away from that slot machine. You are so sure that one more quarter would have been the winning one. That was the feeling. It was addictive. I felt compelled. I never thought of changing doctors or giving up. I had slot machine syndrome.

It was time for surgery. Why the doctor waited so long to do this, I do not know, but it was finally suggested that a laparoscopy be performed. This minor surgical procedure is devised to take a look inside your body and see if there's any blockage in the fallopian tubes that would stop the egg from dropping down and entering the uterus. The procedure is simple, but it does have to be done in the hospital. An apparatus is put through the belly button which has a camera at the very end of it and it is probed down the fallopian tubes. If the camera doesn't detect any blockage, it is withdrawn, you get a band-aid and are sent home. If blockage is found, they proceed right then and there with surgery. The doctor and I had agreed that if they discovered something, they would perform the surgery necessary to open up the fallopian tubes and clear a passage. If that were the case, I would be hospitalized for about a week.

As is true with many surgeries and as was for me, I didn't know what to hope for. On the one hand, I wanted them to find nothing wrong so I could keep trying and soon drop the winning quarter. On the other hand, I very much wanted them to find something so I'd finally identify a problem which they could fix, and I could move on towards success. We had been at this for years. It was demoralizing and expensive. It was taking an enormous toll on every aspect of my life. Being hopeful and then let down every single month was the worst part.

They certainly found something when they went through with those cameras.

They found a wall of scar tissue. Scar tissue that had been building every year that the IUD had been in my body; all that time I had complained to the doctor of pain and questioned why I was bleeding so heavily; scar tissue had been building and building to the point an egg could never move down my fallopian tubes.

As I had agreed, surgery was performed on the spot. They went into the fallopian tubes, in many ways just like a roto-rooter goes into pipes and cleaned out all the scar tissue. The end of the fallopian tubes are these tiny, microscopic, hair-like follicles that capture the egg and drop it where it's supposed to go.

Those follicles were matted and bent and consequently non-functional. The microsurgery pulled them out, follicle by follicle, cleaned them off, straightened them out and rendered them, hopefully, useful. However, the nature of scar tissue is that once it has developed, it grows back very quickly. So, there was only a short window of time through which we had to get pregnant before the scar tissue would start to grow back again.

Although I had consented to the surgery if it was required, one more time, I was completely unprepared for what to expect. Now typical of my entire medical experience, nobody really talked to me about what was going to happen. For instance, nobody told me that when I got out of surgery, there would be an open hole in my body with a rag hanging out of it from which the wound would drain. An open hole, about an inch long, with green drain coming out of it. I expected I'd be back at work fairly quickly, although they did say to expect to be out of work for four weeks. I played down the length of recovery because I've always been the type to work even when I'm sick. I virtually never missed work. I was kind of an animal. But I felt like I had been hit with a Mack truck. I was profoundly disabled by it and in a lot of pain. I remember crying mostly because I was unprepared for it. I had no idea I would have a rope hanging out of me after surgery. It scared the shit out of me. And I didn't know how to clean it; I didn't know what to do with it.

I was home recuperating for a full four weeks. Animal or no animal, I could not go back to the office for four weeks. My boss was wonderful and very supportive. As I began to heal and by the time I was able to go back to work, I started to get excited again. Now everything was cleared, and we knew what the problem had been. We were ready to try again, and the artificial inseminations began. My hope was renewed. All that lost time didn't even seem to matter. We just wanted to get on with it. The first month I got my period. I was okay. I figured what were the odds of it happening the first month. The second month I got my period. I was a little disappointed, but I was still okay. Starting about the third month, then the fourth, then the fifth, then the sixth month, the light of hope became dimmer and dimmer. I realized that the scar tissue was growing back and my chances of getting pregnant were getting smaller and smaller. I kept trying, going each month three times for the inseminations, for probably another year. Same as before. Sometimes my period was late and I almost always thought I was pregnant. It was endless highs and lows. Insemination high, getting my period low. Up and down and up and down.

We had arrived at a point when it was time to take a good, hard look at ourselves; a look at what was going on with me and my body and make a decision about what we were going to do. It was time to accept the fact that I wasn't going to get pregnant. It wasn't going to happen. I needed to accept that fact and decide.

CHAPTER 4

Putting Reproduction Behind

We reached the point of knowing that we would never have a child of our own. I accepted it. In order to move on, I had to accept it.

Throughout the whole process of trying to get pregnant, irritating as it was at times, demeaning, infuriating and painful as it was at times, I never, ever, thought I wasn't going to get pregnant. I just thought it was something I had to get through before my luck would hit. It was inconceivable and unfathomable that I would not get pregnant. And the realization now that it was never going to be was like losing your best friend. It was like losing a part of yourself that you take as much for granted as you take the movement of your arms and legs. For many women, being a mother must be something akin to her own fingerprint. As much a part of her as that.

Giving up was hard for me. In my work and in life, I was nothing if not tenacious. An almost scary tenacity. I just didn't stop. Nothing could stop me. If you said no, I would work to change your no into a yes. And often did. But I couldn't change my body. All the tenacity in the world couldn't change the fact that I couldn't get pregnant. I ultimately wasn't able to prevail, and I wanted to move on from the sadness and growing bitterness. It was time to let go.

CHAPTER 5

Facing the Options

IN OUR MIND AT THE TIME, there was only one option. Private adoption. Jim and I made the decision that we would adopt a child and we made an appointment with an attorney.

In Los Angeles, there are a handful of attorneys whose names are the ones offered up over and over by "people in the know" who handle private adoption. Our first meeting was with one of them. We were brought into his office and asked to sit down. Jim and I were very nervous, holding hands very tightly. We never imagined when we first got married that we would find ourselves in a situation like this. But that was not the first time, nor the last, that we had that feeling.

The attorney's manner was particularly brusque and unpleasant. He very matter-of-factly presented us with the statistics: "You have a twenty percent chance of this; you have a sixty percent chance of that. There is a long list of couples wanting to adopt." The meeting ended with his saying, "I'm going to leave my office now. When I return, if you have left a check for $5,000 on my desk, I will put you at the top of the list and get you a baby within three months." Then he left the room. We were so thrown — our hands were shaking; our legs were wobbly. A credible, famous Beverly Hills attorney. We didn't leave $5,000; we just left. It saddens me to think of how many desperate couples, just like us, must have left the money on his desk, no questions asked.

Still, life being the imperative that it is, once we recovered from that, we made an appointment with another attorney. I was given the name of Steven Rabin, who came highly recommended. In a meeting that went on for at least three hours, we were guided through common adoption procedure. With his counsel, we were to write an ad and place that ad in several newspapers in American states that have a proven track record of attracting larger numbers of women with unwanted pregnancies. The ads were supposed to say something along the lines of: "Desperate couple wanting to give love and care to a child. If you're looking for adoptive parents, please call us." The best results, we were told, came from placing these ads in places like Montana, Kansas, and the American South. A high occurrence of teenage pregnancy is particularly prevalent in these areas of the country and often these young women were opposed to abortion or often of a mind or need to give up their "unwanted" children. In other areas of the country, the "success" rate declines substantially. Considering which particular cultural group may be more inclined to give up an unwanted child was also suggested to us. In some pockets of culture, adoption is a more acceptable solution.

For me, this already began to have an uncomfortable, exploitative feeling about it.

It felt like we would be trolling the waters for desperate young women in areas where they're comparatively disadvantaged and perhaps less educated. While the attorney talked about areas that were more fruitful for getting children, I couldn't help but feel that this wasn't good for the women from whom they were getting the children. It bothered me; it deeply bothered me.

I feel it is important to say that this was my particular reaction. I know that for many of these women who find themselves pregnant and unable to care for a child, a couple offering a loving home to raise this child is extraordinary. In many, many cases, I believe putting these couples and birthmothers together is a miraculous and life-saving connection. It's a solution that works for all parties.

It just felt very uncomfortable for me, and it wasn't just my concern for the pregnant young women. It was also my reservations and fear about the physical condition of the birthmothers. Drug use now is so pervasive, and the long term emotional and physical disabilities which result are only just beginning to be understood. It was around this time that Jill Ireland had come forward with her story. She and Charles Bronson adopted a child from birth. He grew into a terribly disturbed boy who eventually committed suicide. In this particular case, the boy's birthmother had been a drug addict, which Jill Ireland was not aware of when the adoption took place. She discovered that later on. Rightly or wrongly, Jill Ireland suspected strongly that her child suffered his whole life because of the excessive drugs taken during pregnancy. There is a growing certainty in the medical community that excessive drug and alcohol use by a pregnant woman can cause lifelong emotional and psychological problems in their offspring. What biologically, physically, emotionally would be the story with this child?

Adopting a baby from a young woman that I didn't know, I remembered all the things I did to my body when I was young, particularly how reckless I could be with my health. In most cases, adoptive parents would know nothing of the history of the father. The attorney explained to us that in over eighty percent of these situations, the boy or man who got the woman pregnant is long gone from the picture. I was uncomfortable with all of this.

Additionally, we were instructed by the lawyer to get a separate phone line and to use a script when the prospective birth mother called. This separate telephone number would be only for responses to our newspaper ad and when we picked up the phone we should be prepared. We were asked to leave the script by the phone and it too was written with a formula which would bring about the best results. It would also be useful in case we froze when we picked up the phone. We were shown a sample letter and asked to write something similar that would be sent to anyone responding to our ad. With the letter, we were told to include a photograph of Jim and me standing in front of our house. If we had a dog or cat, it should be in the picture, preferably in my arms. And in the letter, we were to talk about how desperate we were, how long we had been waiting for a baby, how much we wanted to care for a baby. We were asked to describe our yard and what kinds of toys we'd provide for a child.

Like so many other aspects of my quest for a baby, this was humiliating. And as I've described, it also felt manipulative.

Again, it's important to make the point that I recognize what a miracle private adoption is for so many people and how many successful, happy, rewarding unions have been made in choosing this route.

But my reaction ran deep, and I didn't think I could do it.

CHAPTER 6

Choosing Surrogacy

To this day, I can't remember how it is that we came to consider surrogacy as a possibility. But at some point, it moved from something that was not even an option to a possibility we were considering.

We had been told about the "Center for Surrogacy," located right here in Los Angeles, California. I have since learned that people come to the Center from all over the country, in fact, from all over the world. That is because surrogacy is illegal in most states, but not in California. It is owned and run by Bill Handel. We made an appointment. We were struck immediately by what a thorough and professional organization he ran. During the course of our meeting, we talked with a psychologist, medical doctors, an attorney, and we talked with Bill Handel himself.

There was a quality about this organization that seemed far less exploitative. The majority of the opposition to surrogate adoption, by feminists in particular, is on the grounds that it is highly exploitative. Their argument is that surrogacy is about rich women using the bodies of poor women to get their children. I define myself as a feminist and had a very different reaction. For me, it felt far more deceitful to go after these young women all over the country, who find themselves at a point of crisis in their young lives, pregnant and carefully directed to couples with money who put ads in the newspaper to attract these young women. It seemed opportunistic to write letters convincing them that they are the couple the woman should choose.

Of course, for many, many people private adoption can be the perfect solution for the pregnant woman and the childless couple. But for me, I couldn't shake that feeling that this was underhanded, whereas surrogacy was a choice made voluntarily by the woman herself; it was an event created with her own free will.

The women who came to the Center for Surrogacy came because they wanted to. They weren't women who suddenly found themselves in a bad spot, pregnant with an unwanted child; the surrogates were there because they wanted to be there, because they chose to be there. Many of these women, Bill told us, often shared a similar life situation. They frequently were older, usually married, and always with children of their own. Many were screened very carefully by a team of psychologists to ensure that their motivations in doing this were for the right reasons. The Center was not looking for women who wanted to do this just for money but rather who had a powerful desire to make a difference in somebody's life.

Women who wanted to make nothing short of a miracle for somebody and as unbelievable as it may sound, there are actually a lot of women who do. These are also women who get pregnant very easily, who enjoy being pregnant, and who come to the

Center very aware that there are many women who suffer with infertility and they have an incredible, life-changing gift they can offer to a couple.

If we worked together with a surrogate, it would be my husband's sperm that would impregnate her, thereby creating a baby at least partly genetically our own. I think this made more of a difference to Jim than it did to me, but it is an aspect of surrogate adoption that felt so desirable to us. When we left the Center for Surrogacy, it occurred to us that this might be our answer and we began to consider it seriously.

Shortly thereafter, we heard about a woman named Nina Kellog who was a psychologist in private practice. Nina arranged both private and surrogate adoptions. We heard good things about her too and we scheduled a meeting.

She was a warm, kind woman whose whole life and work revolved around children. She had children of her own, but they were all grown and out of the house. Her office was plastered with dozens and dozens of pictures of babies. Babies were her thing. Nina was a woman with a mission and that was to get babies into homes of people who were absolutely unambivalent about being parents and who were ready and eager to devote everything to their children. She loved what she did, and we loved Nina. She explained that she used to be a partner of Bill Handel, but at a point, realized that they wanted to approach the business of adoption differently and went their separate ways. He built the Center for Surrogacy, a big building in Beverly Hills and she had a small office in West L.A. We told Nina our story and talked with her about surrogate adoption. She described the process. She would find the surrogate; she would interview the surrogate. The possible surrogate would interview us. It would be her responsibility to make sure that the person she brought to us had the right motivations; that she was a healthy and mature person, motivated by a desire to help a couple who have long awaited a child. The fact that the surrogate would earn ten thousand dollars was not insignificant to many of them, but it was not their primary motivation. Nor should either party be faulted for the fact that money was indeed a part of this. A woman who becomes a surrogate is giving, along with many other things, her time and it is reasonable and fair that she be paid for that.

Once the surrogate had been found and we all agreed to work together, then Nina's job would be to offer weekly counseling sessions with the surrogate. These sessions provided a place for surrogates to discuss concerns of friends or family who may disapprove, to share excitement when the surrogate became pregnant, and to support each other on a group level. Nina would find the obstetrician that the surrogate would use for the inseminations and an attorney to represent the surrogate. She would be responsible for guiding us all through these steps.

Nina was already working with a whole group of couples and their pregnant surrogates. This was unbelievable to us. We were now talking <u>baby</u>. This wasn't about medicine, or surgery, or endless doctor's visits. We were talking about an actual baby. In all the years I had been going to the doctor's, it was all about my body and what was wrong with it; it was never about actual pregnancy. Many times, we had lost hope that we would ever be talking about a real baby.

CHAPTER 7

Llana

I WILL NEVER FORGET THIS. Preparing for our initial meeting with the woman who might actually be our surrogate and thinking about its colossal importance, I realized the import and effect this meeting and possible ensuing relationship would have on me, perhaps for the rest of my life. I thought of everything that was riding on it. In preparing for the meeting, I was beyond sick. When I say sick (and you will hear it a lot) what I mean is an apocalyptic dread and fear. I was agitated, nervous, and nauseous. I must have tried on every single outfit in my closet. Put it on, looked at it, no, I look too severe. Another outfit, put it on, no, I look stupid. Another outfit, put it on, no, I don't look maternal, I don't look like a loving person in this. Take it off.

Part of this, as you can imagine, is trying to present yourself to somebody and appear worthy enough for them to like you enough and think you're worthwhile enough for them to agree to do this for you. Also remember that there are two thousand couples waiting for every available baby in Los Angeles right now — that's why waiting lists at adoption agencies are four- and five-year waits. Llana would probably meet many couples and she could decide for whom she wanted to do this. There were a lot of people who would be prepared to beg Llana to do this for them. In my mind, <u>everything</u> was riding on this meeting.

I felt terribly old. I was worried that she would not want to do it because we were too old. So that was the other factor. I wanted to look fresh and motherly.

And I was looking haggard and terrified!

I was nervous about the meeting. I wanted to have a glass of wine to calm myself down before the meeting. I thought I couldn't do that because if she smelled alcohol on my breath, she would think I was a drunk and a loathsome creature. And she would never agree to have a baby for us. I drove around the area several times before I parked the car. My heart was beating so hard that I could barely breathe. I never had such performance anxiety in my life.

I met Jim before we actually had the meeting. We lunched at the Hamlet Gardens and that was when I deeply wanted the glass of wine. I would have given my soul for the calming effect I would get from a glass of wine, but I didn't do it. I didn't know what might affect her; what might create a good impression or a bad impression. I don't recall Jim and me saying very much; I was hyperventilating most of the lunch. Jim was anxious too, and he's a pretty relaxed guy.

We drove over to Nina's office. At that point we were so sick we couldn't even talk to each other. We were zombified on the way to the office. And I wasn't having a good hair day. My hair was flat, and I was very upset about that! And my hands... I was worried about my hands. Worried that she might see that

I bite my nails. I wanted to project this calm, loving, maternal, worthwhile person.

When you're put in a situation like this, even though I'm able to joke a little about it now, there is an element that is deeply upsetting. This is so hard to say because I know one should be so grateful for the opportunity to go into a meeting like this; so grateful that you might have this chance. That this woman is willing just to meet you and talk to you about it. You should be excited and you should be grateful. But I also felt — and I had to repress it and swallow it because it felt very inappropriate — anger at having to be put in this position. Not at the woman I was about to meet, but by life. Of having to present myself this way to be judged whether I was worthy or not worthy; whether I was likeable or not likeable. And it just fanned the flames of all kinds of emotional havoc. I was repressing the feelings because they didn't feel appropriate and I didn't feel entitled to them but I did, nonetheless, feel enraged at having to be put in this position.

A lot of things were jumbled up together — excited, worried, delighted, and angry. That was the part of this situation that I didn't talk to anybody about. I was ashamed of those feelings and I didn't really even admit them to myself a lot of the time. But I would be dishonest if I didn't say that parallel to all of the expected feelings of excitement and gratitude to this wonderful woman was this surprising upsurge of resentment of being put up on a block like this to be deemed acceptable or not acceptable by a stranger. And I hated myself and my body for having so failed me.

We got to the office and Jim and I were both very, very nervous. We walked into the waiting room and instead of Nina being there when we walked in, Llana was sitting there alone. So, we arrived at this momentous encounter, entered the waiting room without Nina there to help us — to make an introduction — to say anything — to be a buffer — to be a helper. We were left on our own. Jim made some lame joke about it certainly being a strange sensation to meet the mother of my child — which just kind of laid there. Llana was very calm. I remember looking at her and staring at her features: her hair color, her hands, and thinking that these traits would be passed on to my child. I saw that she was very pretty.

She was blonde; my hair is dark brown, and my skin olive toned.

I wanted to talk to Llana. I wanted to show Llana what was inside my heart. I felt instinctively that if I could tell her everything we had been through, telling her how long we had waited to have a child, that my experiences would be meaningful to her. She would respond to them because she was a woman and she had a child of her own. But even more than my desire to let Llana know me, was my more intense interest in her and to know all about this woman who made such an extraordinary decision to be a surrogate. I was grateful when Llana initiated the conversation. She was totally open and extremely interested in me knowing who she was and what brought her to that office that day.

Llana talked about her little girl and how deeply meaningful and important her daughter Allana was. I think Allana was about three years old then, maybe a little bit younger. Llana proudly talked about this child and showed pictures to Jim and me of this little girl. She talked about the relationship that she had with her and how satisfying it was to be in the world, on her own, with her daughter.

She made it clear that she was not interested in meeting another man. She was very intent on letting us know that she, under no circumstances, ever wanted to have another child for herself. She wanted us to understand the nature of the connection that she had to Allana and how disruptive she felt it would be if there was another child in the house. She emphasized her devotion to Allana, recognizing it to be unique. In fact, there were no other major human commitments or attachments in her life except this daughter. She was very clear that she would never change her mind and keep the baby she was having for us; she didn't want to have anything interrupt the dyad.

She told us that she had met a woman who had suffered with infertility for a long time. She had seen firsthand the damage the infertility caused — the effect that the total experience had on her. She couldn't help but think quietly to herself from time to time, "God, I could do this for her. I could easily have this baby for her."

She said that she got pregnant very easily. "When I decided to have a child", she told me, "I told my lover and we had intercourse for the purpose of making a child. I got pregnant right away, I'm sure that it would happen again. I'm young, I'm healthy, I haven't had relationships with any men since then, but I feel quite sure I would get pregnant right away. And I would like to do this for somebody. I would particularly like to help in this kind of a way because of the magnitude of changes I could make for someone. I have no desire to keep the child. The last thing I would do is to bring a child into our home because of what I've already told you about Allana and me."

I listened intently to her, but I was watching her even more closely. It's a bizarre moment where you meet face to face the person who might actually be the mother of a baby who will come into your life and who will be with you for so many years, perhaps be with you for the rest of your life. I couldn't help watching her hands and looking at her teeth and her hair and her bone structure, her face and her body, thinking that a child who I would hold in my arms and love and patch up when their knees got scraped, and sweat through the night with them before the senior prom, and all of those things that you do with your children, that the child would look like her in some way. It's almost a dream-like state when you're in the room watching and listening, not to mention all the other unreal aspects of a conversation of this nature.

I talked a little about how long we had waited, but she knew that. I liked her enormously and answered her questions as honestly as I could. I told her of the feeling of sadness and alienation I had as a child, as how much I have learned in my life that would help to make me a compassionate mother.

I had to take just a leap of faith that there was something she was going to like about me as a person. All of the dread and fear that I had prior to that meeting really revolved around her deciding if I was going to be good enough, whether she'd think I was worthy of her sharing this experience with her, of her sharing her body to help us.

When we left Nina's office that day, Jim and I left having no idea of how we did.

Usually if you have a job interview and you leave the job interview, you more or less know. I blew this totally, or I did well. I'll probably get the job, or I probably won't. We had no idea whether we did well or not.

I could not read Llana at all. She had a kind of reserve about her that was outside of my upbringing and life experience. I guess I find myself mostly with people who are like me. What they feel on the inside is pretty much fully exposed in some revealing way on the outside for the whole world to see. Whether you want to show it or not, it's hanging out there! There's usually no gray area.

Llana had a reserve about her that I wasn't used to. Which is not to say that she was cold because she wasn't at all. There was just not a great display of feeling. But she was very sweet, in many areas quite open, but her behavior was controlled. On some level, we also appreciated that because we didn't want this to turn into an orgy of emotion, letting feelings get out of control only to be hurt in the end if Llana chose not to be a surrogate for us. Among all of the other high emotion and genuine drama, this also was a professional transaction and that's how, in certain ways, she behaved. Not exclusively, because she fully felt a real mission to become pregnant for a childless couple. Money was definitely not Llana's motivation, but she was handling our meeting in a professional way; she went about it in a somewhat subdued way.

So, because of that, when we left, we had no idea where we stood. I didn't know if she loved me, I didn't know if she hated me, I didn't know if she couldn't wait to get hold of me to tell me she was going to do it or if she was right then and there, sticking her finger down her throat and saying to Nina, "get them away from me, don't ever let them call me, I don't want to see them, keep them away from me, I hate you for introducing me to them!" We didn't know.

We went home to be sick for a few more hours, staying in our house waiting for a call. And that was the way our life was going to go. About eight that evening, the phone rang. We had two lines. Jim had an office and I had my own phone. She called on Jim's line. We heard the phone ring and our hearts were beating out of our chests and there was no more breathing. Not an inhale; not an exhale. We were hovering over the machine and we heard Nina's voice. Jim picked up and we knew this was it. There was no oxygen in the room. We waited. Nina said, "Llana wants to do it for you. She liked you both, felt connected to you, and she really wants to do this for you. She understood exactly where you were coming from, she thinks that you have a good sense of her, and she wants to go forward with you." We were thrilled (I almost passed out), enormously grateful, and intensely happy. Now we couldn't breathe again, but this time it was from indescribable joy.

We let those feelings surge pleasantly for about five minutes because now we knew that the Mary Beth Whitehead journey was about to begin. Then, we moved directly to being terrified. We wondered anxiously, after all of this, if she indeed got pregnant and we assumed that she would, what if she changed her mind?

How can anybody really know how they'll feel when the baby is born? Mary Beth Whitehead was also completely adamant she wouldn't want to keep the baby. What if Llana, despite all her sureness now, changed her mind a few days, weeks, months, or even years after the baby was born? We went from fear that she was going to reject us, to ecstasy that she chose us, to terror that she was going to withhold the baby.

The next phase moved us towards Llana's attorneys. We felt insecure and nervous because the legal aspect of her changing her mind was the fear of being hurt in a way that was so profound that you believe you would never recover. I sincerely believed that if I went through this experience with her and she got pregnant, deciding at the very last minute to keep the baby, that I'd be hurt beyond repair. An even worse fear was that she would take the baby back after we got him home. I suspected that I would not recover from that. There are only a couple of things in this life that would devastate me. Not many because I am quite resilient. I don't think I could ever recover from being raped, for example. I just don't think I could. I think that it would change my life and I'm not sure I could have recovered from finally getting this baby only having to give it up after it was born and home with me.

Llana came to Nina through a woman named Barbara Sherwin, an attorney, who was married to a man who was also her partner. These details and transactions scared us during the process. It could be little things like Llana didn't want to go to the doctor that Nina wanted her to go to. The Sherwins encouraged her to choose her own doctor, not Nina's. The doctor that Nina worked with is one of the most famous and well-respected OB-GYN's in Los Angeles in addition to being one of the kindest hearted doctors I've ever met. But the Sherwins nixed him and pushed Llana to another doctor unknown to Nina or Jim and me. If she chose her own doctor, which she ultimately did, we wouldn't know where this doctor stood on the questions of surrogacy. The majority of doctors in Los Angeles will not handle surrogates. They will not inseminate women who want to be surrogates. They will have nothing to do with them because of the potential lawsuits. They just won't do it. It's very, very hard to find a doctor to work with you. We didn't even know if she told the doctor that she was going to be a surrogate. It was out of our hands and out of our control. A very scary process.

Again, let's say she got pregnant. Let's say the doctor found out she was pregnant in her first trimester and began to counsel her that she should not give the baby up. What if he was really opposed to it? What if he was religiously opposed to it? We didn't know. And it wasn't my body. I didn't have control. Any woman who already had lost control over her body to the degree that infertility renders you, every additional situation of that nature further intensifies that feeling of helplessness.

Llana wanted to work with the Sherwins as her attorneys. Rightfully and ethically, she had to have her own attorney, not ours, but we were to pay their fee. This is how it's done, and we had no problem with that. But there was a drama going on with the Sherwins. Barbara Sherwin was jealous and very critical of Nina. Nina explained to us the bond between her and Llana was vital to this whole experience. This was going to be a long process. It usually takes about six months to get pregnant and then, of course, there's nine months of pregnancy.

The surrogate really needs to have a safe place to vent and to discuss things. That place was with Nina. Surrogate mothers have found it comforting and fun to be in a group with other surrogates, sharing the same experience. Also, counseling might provide a sounding board to be able to work through any feelings that may come up. Often times, the surrogate feels fine, but is constantly fielding objections, criticism, and sometimes well-meaning disbelief from friends and acquaintances. If Llana's view of Nina was devalued, the basic confidence a surrogate should feel for the leader would erode and the whole experience could easily become jeopardized. One of the most satisfying aspects of the surrogate's experience, aside from bringing a baby to a couple, are the friendships she makes within the group. Very often these friendships continue long after the adoption takes place.

Barbara was trying to get Llana away from Nina for two reasons. One, and she told this to Llana, she hated Nina because she said years ago, Nina tried to steal her husband. Unbelievably, this information was told to Llana. This was obviously unethical and immoral to say these things to a woman who had committed herself to this process with Nina. Barbara also had ambitions to start her own surrogate program and she had hopes that Llana would leave Nina and be a surrogate for the Sherwins. This could have easily put us out of the picture.

Llana could at any point say, "you know what, I'm not going to deal with Nina." A phone call was all it would have taken for her to say, "I'm sorry, but I'm going to go with Barbara and we're going to start again." That's all it would have been.

Ten seconds and it would have been over. I don't think we would have gone through with it. I don't think we could have allowed our expectations to be raised only for another disappointment. We couldn't bear that Barbara could upset the delicate equilibrium. Her actions were unethical. She was way out of line in these kinds of conversations, not to mention infantile and mean-spirited.

I got Barbara on the phone and I said, "God, please, please, please, Barbara, don't do this. We have been through a lot. Please be careful about what you say to Llana. We're all so vulnerable now. This is supposed to go a certain way. She's supposed to be connected to Nina. If you say these unconscionable things about Nina, it's unfair. You're really disrupting a delicate balance. You can understand that. Please don't undermine her relationship with Nina. We've started with Nina and Llana's working well with her. Don't do that to us. Please. If you're going to stay involved as her attorneys, fine. Support her legally, the way you're supposed to, but please don't involve yourself in these other matters."

She continued, unwittingly or purposely, to disrupt Llana's attachment to Nina all the way through the process until the contracts were finally signed. The Sherwins then submitted a bill to us for five thousand dollars.

At one point, after the contracts were signed, just before we began the inseminations, Nina told me that Llana had expressed some confusion about the ovulation predictor test; she wasn't really clear about how to use the thermometer, in order to chart the temperature. Nina suggested that we should carefully go over it with her. I functioned almost like a big sister might to a younger sister.

Pregnancy is a very scientific and tedious process. When going through it myself, I had to nail that temperature on the day it goes up a tenth of a degree. You can only get pregnant one day a month. If she couldn't read the thermometer, it might extensively delay the process. And I was impatient and deeply uneasy.

The contracts are signed and now Nina has set up her group meetings with Llana. We're beginning to move towards the first insemination and Llana's not sure about how to do the ovulation predictor. We decide we'll have a meeting. We hadn't met her daughter Allana yet. Liana would like us to meet Allana. It was Valentine's day, I remember, because we brought Allana a gift. Just the four of us would go to this restaurant. Because I wanted to bring a gift to Allana, I went to the toy store, the first time we'd been in a toy store since I was a child.

Being childless and having steered away from people with children, I was a clueless person in a toy store, and I was totally intimidated by it. By the way, whenever I was around anything to do with children, I held my breath. So, I was kind of hyperventilating in this store. It was part nervousness, it was part excitement, it was part of a general sickness. I went into the store and was somehow able to get a voice out to ask for help and said, "what does a three- year old girl like?" I had no idea. Like a person from another planet, I was brought to an aisle and shown some general things. I agonized about should I get a big, wonderful gift or will that appear as if we're these horrible rich people? Or if I purchased a sweet, small gift, will it backfire, making us seem cheap? I wasn't able to breathe.

The gift and the tormenting experience of buying it illustrates the road ahead of me! I obsessed over this gift. God help me for the long run. Finally, I got the gift. It was a nail polish thing, but it was not the gift I wanted to get. I was upset. In the car, I was self-critical. I made the wrong choice and I knew it! When we got to the restaurant, I had brought the ovulation predictor kit, yet I feared I had the gift and it was wrong. And no breathing.

The restaurant had a lot of stairs. I was gripped in a state of almost chronic anxiety for a very long time. There was so much riding on this meeting, at least I felt there was. I blew everything out of proportion, getting a gift for this three- year old child could almost put me in the hospital. A conversation about the ovulation predictor put me in a state of medical alert! I exaggerated the situation, knew was exaggerating it, but I couldn't help myself.

So, we sat there. Would I let myself drink? No. I was afraid she would think I was an alcoholic and I would not drink. Despite my discomfort and my breathing problem, I wouldn't even permit myself a glass of wine. She didn't order one.

She probably thought the same thing.

Then we met her daughter. This is kind of laughable, but we had not been around children. We were people who have not been around children at all and were not attuned or responsive to kids. We were stiff and stupid. We had difficulty establishing a rapport with this child. We didn't know how to make conversation. We were totally outside the universe of children, ill-at-ease, and ill-informed of what to talk about. My basic questions were: How old are you? Do you like your teacher? That began and ended my conversational repertoire of being with a child.

But she was a three-year old, anyhow, and thank God, went roaming the restaurant. She didn't stay at the table very much. I thought that was odd at the time. Now I realize her mother was just lucky that she stayed within the confines of the restaurant at all.

The subject of the ovulation predictor came up. I said, "you know, I had a lot of trouble with this (which was true) when I went through all of these inseminations and the kits are very difficult to read. They're very tough and they were the bane of my existence. Let me show you what I did and how I worked with it, because the instructions require you have to have a Ph.D. to understand them."

These instructions were very convoluted, with tiny type and difficult to grasp.

We went through it together in the restaurant. I held my breath and left the restaurant in a state of concern. I was unbelievably preoccupied with it. (Just put the word sick in as a constant for the next few years) And I do mean it. The people who knew me then, like my assistant, Sue, knew how flipped out I was. You actually spend more time with people you work with than the people you live with. Sue was a wonderful, empathetic friend. A wonderful young woman whom I confided in every day. We never got a lick of work done until all of the surrogacy information was passed on and processed. She was very close to me, knowing everything. Sue was a great friend and a great support.

We did the first insemination, done strictly by the book. Jim went to a doctor's office and produced a specimen into a cup. The doctor's office transported the specimen to Llana's doctor. Llana's doctor inseminated her. And we waited what seemed like an interminable period. We were now really back in the game. Waiting. We realized that people never get pregnant the first month. We knew that statistically. But we thought, "she could get pregnant. She said she got pregnant right away with her first child." Wish overwhelmed the real probabilities. We speculated, it's certainly more than possible. We waited, but she didn't get pregnant.

She told us that she really didn't like going to the doctor for the insemination. She remained unsure about the whole ovulation thing. Llana said to me that she preferred for Jim to come to her apartment and give the sperm to her. She would then insert it herself with a syringe. We were very uneasy about that proposal, thinking that it lacked a certain clinical aspect. But Nina, being very relaxed, advised that it would be fine. Llana would probably be more relaxed, it'll be easier for her, she doesn't have to leave her child, which is hard to do.

Nina endorsed the change. That began a period of several months were Jim would, when she called to say she was ovulating, produce the specimen at home in a cup, and get in his car and drive over to her apartment. He would take the cup in the car to her house, bring it to her door, give it to her, say goodbye and leave. Sometimes, he produced the specimen at her apartment. Jim jokes that he developed quite an erotic attachment to cups. To this day, he can't really look at a cup the same way.

It just didn't feel real because it wasn't in a doctor's office and I was worried sick about it. Nina felt comfortable with the arrangement, saying that Llana was doing great. Llana emerged a leader in the group, the other women looked up to her. There was something about Llana that was solid. She knew who she was. She had a coherent view of herself in the world. That's a trait to aspire to: to have confidence about who you were, where you were, where you're going, what your beliefs were. Llana was a clear-thinking person and very accomplished as a writer. She aspired to do many more things in the future. And I was sure she would succeed.

For several months, the same situation occurred, recalling the years when I was artificially inseminated. You get so excited. The day comes and you do the insemination, then you do another one, then another and then you wait. These two weeks go by so slowly. Then the phone call from Llana. She got her period. The worst is the next two weeks — waiting for the next ovulation.

But we were determined: we kept going. Llana so thoroughly and completely wanted to do this for us that she exuded confidence. Her voice implied that she could pull it off right away. When we got the telephone call announcing her period, I could hear plainly a flat, deep disappointment. Surprise and disappointment. Deep disappointment that she was letting us down. She expressed astonishment that it wasn't happening.

We came to know her menstrual schedule. We'd know after the insemination how many days we had to count for the critical telephone call. One day... the telephone call didn't come. We didn't even speak of it so as to not jinx it. Jim and I didn't say, "hey, she didn't call today." We both thought it, but we didn't utter a word. The next day came. No telephone call. We didn't say anything then either. It was so heavy with possibilities of the highest joy and the saddest disappointment that we refused to speak of it. Then another day passed and we said, "hey, she's three days late." This was a first.

Even though we didn't want to acknowledge it, even though we told ourselves not to raise our hopes, the excitement was starting to build. We called her. We said, "h-e-l-l-o-o-o?" She said, "h-e-l-l-o-o-o?" We said, "have we counted right? Are you three days late?" She said, "yes, I am. What should I do?" I said, "do you want to take a home pregnancy test?" She said, "okay." She went to the store, purchased one, requiring that you test the morning urine. We had an uneasy night of no breathing, no talking, no nothing. We stayed in the petrified position. It was a long, agitated night.

When the phone rang the next day, it was Nina because Llana called Nina. I think she was supposed to do that. She was pregnant! It was a positive. We flew out of the house. For some reason, we couldn't stay in the house. Because the joy was so tremendous, it didn't fit in the house; it couldn't be contained. We literally had to get into a bigger space. We walked down our street. It had happened. We were going to have a baby. She was pregnant. It was over. We were going to have a baby.

We started to talk about baby's names. We started wondering about the sex of the baby. We were as light as air. We were ecstatic to a degree that I hadn't yet experienced in my life.

The joy was indescribable. We began to act like expectant parents. I told Sue. We cried, taking off the whole day. We walked around the streets, picking names for babies. It was an amazing, expansive sensation. Llana was going to go to her doctor, but the initial test had been very clear. She went to the doctor and it was a definite positive. We were launched.

Before and during the time that we were waiting for Llana to get pregnant, my career had continued to grow. It boomed. With that came a tremendous sense of pride, self-regard, and enjoyment. It also brought with it a lot of stress and responsibility as well as very long hours. My day started early in the morning, going until very late at night. I often worked six days a week, sometimes seven.

If this job was preoccupying and demanding, it was one that I loved and valued. It caused me great anxiety, but I was deeply invested in it and it meant a lot to me. I had arrived in a place, in an arena, where I was accomplished and successful.

The success was particularly comforting while I suffered such losses during the extended infertility period and while I felt like a failure for not being able to do something as simple as to be pregnant. While I suffered that, this other success generated by my own ability was there for me to see and to experience. It was extremely meaningful. It also was very tiring. I was traveling a lot and I was getting very worn out.

There was a healthy and significant part of me that felt like this baby was coming in the nick of time. I had accomplished a lot of what I had set out to do. It had been extremely important to me, but its significance was waning in a way that a baby was going to be meaningful. What I wanted more than anything in the world now was to channel the energy and ability that I had that made for this success in my work and pour it into being a mother. I was prepared to invest the time into mothering, to make the effort into being a parent. Mothering would hold different rewards; it would not be a salary; it would not be what size office I had, but something that now was very meaningful to me, namely the health and well-being of a human being. I was very ready to do that and wanted to do that.

I didn't tell anybody at work about my imminent motherhood, just Sue, and a couple of very close women friends that worked with me in the sales force, but none of the management at American Express knew in New York. I had no idea what they were going to think if their publisher was going to have a baby. It was way too soon to talk to them about it. At this point, there were still very few women in positions like mine. I was a publisher and officer in the company, and they were counting on me. My bosses were all men and I didn't know what they would think. I wasn't thinking about that at this point, instead I focused on the baby, my exhilaration and delight about that.

One morning, I came into the office. I had two appointments out. I had left early in the morning and gone to one appointment, then gone to the other appointment and returned to the office,

I think about eleven and twelve in the morning. Once back to my office, I saw Sue sitting inside of my office as opposed to outside of my office where her area was. I saw her and said, "hi, Sue" and came in and sat down. She looked up at me. She was sitting not behind my desk where I sat but on the other side of my desk. There were two chairs set up for people who came to have meetings. She was sitting in one of them. She looked up at me and I looked at her and I said, "what is it?" I sat down, across from her. She took my hands and she said, "we got a call from Llana." I said, "what?" And she said, "Llana is in the hospital." I said, "what?" She said, "she's bleeding." I repeated, "what?" Sue said, "she's miscarried."

That was my worst moment yet. I never expected that. I expected a lot of other things, but I never expected a miscarriage. I don't know why, but I never did. I expected that she could change her mind, I expected that she might want to keep the baby. I didn't even expect those things because she was being so wonderful, but I thought if tragedy was going to strike, it would look differently. I didn't think this would happen.

As I remember it, she told it to me in three stages. If she had started out with "she's had a miscarriage," it would have been worse. It was terrible the way it was, but it took me those three sentences to grasp what was going on. I wanted to go to the hospital and take care of Llana but at the same time all I wanted to do in the world was roll into a ball. I was so scared and upset for Llana — what was she doing in the hospital? Jim met me at the hospital. It turned out that she didn't just have a miscarriage. She had an ectopic pregnancy, which required emergency surgery, having a fallopian tube removed.

It was like God saying to me, "don't even think about it. Don't even play with the idea because you will never have a child. And if you try, I will slap you back so hard that you will never try again." That was such a clear feeling and message that I was getting. It was such a blow. She had emergency surgery. Her life was threatened by this. I was devastated. I didn't think I could ever get up off the floor after that. Time went by and Llana healed. We were shocked and amazed, but unbelievably, Llana told us that she wanted to keep going, to try again. She absolutely felt confident that she could get pregnant for us. She wanted to do it more than anything. She was not at all put off by the surgery. She needed time to recuperate, but that she wanted to keep going.

We all met with her doctor who said, "well, I'll tell you one thing; that can't happen again…you won't have another ectopic pregnancy. The odds of that happening twice are astronomical. So, if Llana feels like she wants to go forward, I would certainly not counsel her against it. Llana is a one hundred per cent healthy woman in every way." We were so moved by Llana wanting to go forward. Moved by her resilience and her determination. Yet, we were very reticent. I don't think we would have gone on with anybody else. I don't think we would have started again with anybody else. The experiment with surrogacy was over at that point for us. We were not going to go forward. The fact that she wanted to continue coupled with the doctor's sanction, her recovery of her health, we thought, okay, and were amazed at her.

I think, another three or four months went by when we couldn't do anything and then we began to inseminate again. And again, Jim went to her house in the evening and that continued for a long time... again. Again, a positive. It was six months after the tubal pregnancy. But this time, I felt very guarded. I wouldn't even let myself get excited about it. She had a miscarriage very early on. It wasn't a traumatic thing, she just started bleeding, like probably a week or two into it. She was late, she had a positive read on her home pregnancy test, and about seven days later, she started bleeding. Lots of women miscarry, but when you're at this level and the stakes are this high and you're waiting this long, it's not a tragedy, like the first time with Llana. At this point, I wasn't even letting myself get excited. Anyhow, I was kind of numb at this point. I didn't think we were ever going to have a baby. I secretly believed the message I thought God had sent me. I didn't think it was ever going to work.

Anyway, this phase excluded me, it was between Jim and Llana. He was going to her house, providing the sperm. I was, as I said, in a certain numbness.

Well, miracle of miracles, she got pregnant again. This time it took. Weeks went by and there was no miscarriage. And I began to think maybe it was happening. Maybe this was happening. Another telephone call to the office and our hopes totally collapsed. Llana was in the hospital again. Catastrophic news: she did have another ectopic pregnancy. Another emergency surgery. She lost her second fallopian tube. This was after the doctor had said it couldn't happen in a million years. So, there we were...back in the hospital again. Back in the emergency ward again. Deja-vu, with all the horror!

Every step along the way where we went back to working with Llana was because of Llana's indomitable spirit and commitment, her belief and desire to do this for us. Her doctor supported us saying that this was not only okay, but it was inconceivable that it could recur. I just couldn't go anywhere else. This was my last, last hope. I was flattened. It was like I was in a prize fight and I took a blow to the face. And I took another blow in the face and another blow in the face. And forget about me... Llana was sterilized for God's sake.

It was like a giant fist coming out of the heavens and saying, "try it again and next time, I'll kill someone." So, that pretty well did it for me.

We had spent two years with Llana. We had gone through two exuberant, difficult, depleting years. Llana told us over and over that she didn't care about the surgeries; that we were not to feel guilty about her fallopian tubes. She was absolutely adamant about not wanting any more children.

We did not say goodbye. The next Christmas, she came over with Allana to spend the holiday together. We still write to each other. Her career is going beautifully and Allana is thriving.

I'll end this part by saying that I got a call at my office. I wasn't there. It was about eight weeks after Llana's second ectopic pregnancy. There was a message.

Sue scotch taped it to my phone which she did only if it was a special call because I hated to be faced with many messages the moment I came in; she knew to always put them to the side of the phone. The message was from Nina and it said "Don't despair. I've come upon a miracle." It was signed Nina. I felt, oh no, no, no... I don't want to try again. I don't even want to talk about it again. But Nina said we wouldn't be interviewing. There was a woman had been told about us and wanted to help us get a baby. She wanted to immediately. Nina was talking about a woman named Sandra.

CHAPTER 8

Sandra

I READ NINA'S MESSAGE AGAIN. "Don't despair, I've come upon a miracle." On the one hand, I had felt with finality a kind of relief that it was over. I would never have a child and Jim and I would never have a family. I think I stopped believing after Llana's first ectopic pregnancy. I'm not a religious person, but I began to believe with no uncertainty that God had spoken powerfully and if we continued to try, we had only been given a small preview of what might actually befall us. Jim and I never made a conscious decision to stop. We never sat down together and said, "we've gone as far as we can go, let's get on with our lives." My husband never reached the point of despair that I had, but a part of me had died and I had given up. I had no thought of continuing to try. But while that pink sheet of paper rested in my hand, the other half of me pulsated with excitement and anticipation. That message was filled with possibility and hope was alive again. I couldn't wait to get home and show it to Jim.

Jim immediately rallied and wanted to try again. He did not hesitate for a moment. I was struggling with too much heartbreak, too many disappointments, too much fear. "Maybe we shouldn't call back. Maybe we should stop. I just don't think I can do it anymore. Let's give ourselves a chance to heal and move on." But Jim was so bright and unambivalent about being a parent and trying still again spoke to the part of me that could still feel hope. We returned Nina's call.

Nina said she had found a perfect candidate for us. "Her name is Sandra. She's happily married with three of her own children. She's one of the most solid, remarkable women I've ever met." She had told Sandra about us, told her what had recently happened and said Sandra wanted to meet us. She believed this was it.

A meeting was arranged quickly. I was every bit as nervous, every bit as worried, as I had been when we went to meet Llana. I went through all the same emotions again — will she like me? Will she want to do this for us? Will this end in heartbreak? I didn't know if I could live through any more crushing blows the likes of which we had just suffered. I felt fear, and in a strange way, scared for my life. But as much as I wanted to protect myself, the air hung heavy with anticipation and excitement. We arrived at Nina's office.

The first time I set eyes on Sandra I was struck by her radiance. She was one of those rare individuals who beams from within. Her face was open and her eyes were as blue as cornflowers. Her presence was luminescent.

We had a long talk in Nina's office that day. Sandra was there with her husband, Chip. She told us about herself and she wanted to know us. She wanted to know as much about us as possible. She wanted to know about Llana and our feelings about starting a family. We told her everything. It was easy to talk to her. I believed that what brought Sandra to that office was the simple, pure desire to make a miracle for somebody. To take something that had gone horribly awry and fix it. What was motivating Sandra was so clear, so genuine. She was there to help.

She shared with us that she had gotten pregnant before she and Chip were married. They had met as teenagers and fallen in love. They married when they were very young and although sorely tested, as very young marriages with a baby often are, their relationship had survived and strengthened. Their second child was also an unplanned pregnancy, as was their third, but their lives revolved around raising these children and raising them beautifully. Chip and Sandra were committed to each other and committed to their children. I remember Sandra saying that she loved being pregnant; it was a very happy time for her. Chip especially liked her when she was pregnant, and she enjoyed the experience. She said that she got pregnant very easily, which Chip quickly confirmed. Chip actually had a vasectomy after the third child was born. Sandra just got pregnant no matter how careful they were with birth control.

They also talked about the place the church had in their lives. Sandra felt the church was the primary reason they were able to hold their marriage and their family together during those early, difficult days. They talked a lot about their involvement in and the importance of their religion. Sandra was a Christian and very devout in her religious beliefs. But the spiritual tenets by which she lived took a much higher form than a religious label. She was guided by principles rooted in honesty and faithfulness. I admired Sandra's devotion to the church, but it also concerned me. Jim and I are Jewish, and I worried there might be some resistance about choosing a Jewish couple rather than a Christian one. How would the church feel about this? How would she explain this pregnancy? Is what she's doing perceived as immoral? Would she be counseled to abandon the idea? What would she say when confronted by members of the church? Sandra's response was, "I've thought about this and as devoted as I am to my church, I don't think they would understand and rather than having to defend my decision all the time, I think I will probably stop going to church altogether when I begin to show the pregnancy." This statement was so amazing to me from someone who is not only a church goer, but so devoted to the church community and someone who got so much from it. Sandra had made a tremendous choice and was resolved and committed to that choice. I could feel it. It came across with absolute trust and self-assurance and I trusted it. I trusted her.

Chip was very quiet during that first meeting. It was obvious to me that he supported and loved Sandra completely. It is an understatement to say this decision that Sandra had made was quite extraordinary. This road that she was getting ready to walk down was a road not only untraveled by anybody in the world in which she lived, but few in the whole world. And she seemed so resolved, so sure of the choice she had made and her reasons for making it. Chip seemed to take pride in her guts and her willingness to take such a firm stand on something so unpopular in the eyes of many people. Chip was basically a very conservative man and yet he seemed so proud, pleased, and intent on standing by her. And that's exactly what he did.

I learned things about Sandra and Chip that day that earned my respect, my admiration, my confidence, and my trust. I shared with Sandra and Chip, during that meeting, how nervous and anxious I was about everything; how devastating our experience had been for Llana and for us, and how afraid I was that something would go wrong. That was the first time that I saw her do something that I would see many, many, many times throughout our experience together — she kind of just rolled her eyes as if to say, look, we're talking about me getting pregnant and having a healthy pregnancy. If there is one thing in this world I'm absolutely sure of, it's that I can get pregnant and give birth to beautiful, healthy children. You don't have to worry about that. She took pride in, as well she should, how healthy her body was, how easily the pregnancies came, and how smoothly the nine months of the pregnancy went.

Sandra wanted to know a lot about Llana's and our experience. Although there was nothing mean-spirited or competitive about Sandra, she seemed to be very proud of the fact that her body worked so well. She brightened when she said that she knew she would never miscarry; she knew she would get pregnant right away and she knew she would carry the pregnancy to term. Sandra conveyed a calm and assuredness during that meeting which she held throughout the entire experience together. I was terrified at every blink of an eye, every turn of a corner, every cross in the road that we came to. Sandra's repose was both welcome and comforting.

We left that meeting and went home to wait for a telephone call. The call came later that night. Sandra had agreed to be our surrogate. There are no laws in the state of California which govern surrogacy. There are no laws stating that surrogacy is legal or illegal. Legal contracts, although required, frankly are worth nothing. They are unenforceable because there's no guarantee that a surrogate will not change her mind and decide to keep the baby. Jim and I did have the required written contract with Chip and Sandra, but this went way beyond the legalese of any contract. For Sandra and me, this was a bond of two women. A bargain, really, where the stakes are so high; where it all comes down to a promise. A promise that Sandra made to me. It came down to my putting my faith and my trust in Sandra and Sandra trusting me with her body and one of the most momentous decisions of her life. When Sandra called that night, my heart nearly burst with joy and wonder as I listened to her make that promise to me.

We were going to do it and possibility was alive again. This time, Jim and I did not even bother to hire an attorney. Nina made sure, as she was supposed to, that Sandra had her own attorney, but we just had the old contracts retyped and sent to Sandra's lawyer. Everything went through much more easily this time.

Sandra was eager to begin and felt very sure that as soon as she was inseminated that she would get pregnant. She was open to meeting the doctor that Nina had worked with in the past and for whom she had a high regard. His name was Dr. George Weinberger. Sandra fell in love with George and quite honestly, he fell in love with her too. It was understandable. Sandra was so solid, sure of herself, calm, fully aware of the enormity of her undertaking, and all of the connected complexities.

The day came for the first insemination. I wanted to be as close as Sandra would allow throughout the entire experience. It was like a fresh new start for me too. As if I was having my first insemination. Sandra and I went to Dr. Weinberger's together. Jim had done his job by depositing the sperm and had gone back to his office. I stayed in the waiting room while Sandra was inseminated knowing in the most graphic detail everything that was happening to her. When she came out, we looked at each other for a moment... it was possible Sandra was already pregnant. We went to a little restaurant in the medical complex. We were two very different people, coming from different places, feeling our way towards each other and getting to know each other better and more deeply. She talked to me about her children and her husband. We fell into a rhythm of two women working together to create something of great importance. Two women in a unique partnership to make a child. And we talked of little else except that. It wasn't that we weren't interested in the rest of each other's lives. We were. But our focus, what Sandra and I were about, was making a baby.

The first month came and went. And although Sandra was absolutely positive she would get pregnant, she didn't. I was equally positive that not only wouldn't it happen the first month, but because of everything that had happened in the past and even despite how excited Sandra was and how well things were going, it would probably never happen. We got a telephone call from her. Sandra got her period and she was devastated. The confidence she had in her body, her belief that she would become pregnant immediately left her crushed. The same thing happened the second month. We went to the insemination together, stayed together afterwards, and talked about everything we were doing. And then we waited. She called again with her period. Now she was beside herself. I tried to be the voice of reason and calm (which is really the biggest joke in the world) and said, "Sandra, you know, the doctors and Nina say it takes an average of six months. Women often don't get pregnant for at least six months." She said, "Yeah, that may be true for other people, but not me!" I assured her I had every confidence it's going to work and the funny part was, I really did begin to feel confident that Sandra would do it. She would pull it off. We just went forward. When the third month passed and she hadn't gotten pregnant, she was irate at herself, but still very confident.

Jim and I had not taken a vacation together in several years. The job of trying to have a baby superseded any trips away. Between the long hours and stress from my job and the total depletion I felt from the long years of disappointments, I was in a state of exhaustion, depleted mind and body. I had been suffering with chronic back pain for years, due as much to stress as any physical origins. I had lost over ten pounds and was battling nightly insomnia. But because things were going so smoothly, Jim and I thought we just might be able to slip in a long weekend somewhere. We didn't want to go too far from Los Angeles where Sandra would be inseminated, nor did we want to be gone for too long. We decided to go to San Francisco for a long weekend and flew up early on Friday morning. Flying, for me, was painful. Sitting for any length of time without mobility only exacerbated my back pain. But I didn't care. We were going away — for some much needed rest, to escape a long nightmare, and to spend some time together that didn't involve a cup. I bit my lip and got through the flight. I about leapt out of my chair with relief when we landed in San Francisco airport. We got our bags and headed to our beautiful hotel for the weekend.

When we checked in, there was a message waiting for us at the front desk from Sandra. We returned the call before we even put our bags down, while holding our breath. Sandra was home and answered the phone. She called to say she was ovulating. By all calculations, it was at least a week before she was due to ovulate. She had just had her period only about a week earlier. But the ovulation predictor test indicated she was ovulating now. We had encouraged Sandra to start checking her temperature a week or more before she thought she might begin to ovulate, as the variations in degree are so slight and subtle. Sandra, like Llana and like me, found the ovulation prediction test to be intricate and complex. My bathroom used to look like a chemistry lab. I was thinking she must have made a mistake because this was a full week premature. This was not possible. Something was wrong. But… the test said Sandra was ovulating. If we didn't go back immediately the whole month would be lost and it might be six weeks before we could try again. In order not to lose the month, we had to get to the doctor's office today. We picked up our bags, went down to the lobby, grabbed a cab and flew back to Los Angeles.

Several weeks later Sandra telephoned. It was early in the morning and I was dressing for work. She said, "Karen? Is Jimmy home?" I said, "Yes." She said, "Do you want to put him on the line?" Then I couldn't breathe. I screamed for Jim, "Jim, pick-up, pick-up the phone." He got on the phone and she said, "We're pregnant." I said, "Sandra! Sandra, are you sure?" She said, "Yes. I'm sure. I had the lab test done. We're pregnant."

It's difficult to find the words. I was euphoric in listening to her. She was pregnant. The result wasn't from a home pregnancy test, it was from the lab. It was real. I knew that Nina knew because it was Nina who insisted that she go to the lab before she told us. I was elated. Sandra was elated. Jim was elated.

Sandra was pregnant!

We all went to George's for the examination. George did a couple of tests and everything was perfect. Everything was <u>perfect</u>. Sandra was pregnant. She was in ecstasy. She knew she'd get pregnant and she knew she was going to sail through the pregnancy. Although also being beyond deliriously happy, I experienced a heightened state of sickness. Could I have a drip of pleasure from this? No. So little pleasure, so much sickness. My hands were nearly broken from holding them together in excitement. I couldn't breathe. I couldn't believe she was pregnant. The most fearful part of me was so sure that something would go awry. I feared that the hand of God would come out of the sky and smash Sandra down, her husband down, Jim down, me down, take her three children, and then say, "There. Now, try once again if you want to." But above everything, beyond all the neurotic fear was a feeling of such intense happiness and gratitude for Sandra. Whenever I thought of it, of her, I began to cry from joy.

What I didn't know until several days later was that the lab had called Sandra back and said that they couldn't apologize enough but they had given her the wrong result. Her result was negative, not positive. They were really sorry. Sandra was now sick! She had now caught my sickness and was in a sick state herself. The lab called her back again that afternoon and said, "Whoops. We're sorry. It was your test after all. We were wrong the second time we called you. Your result was positive. You are pregnant." Mercifully, we were spared this bit of information for several days. Sandra said the thought of calling me and telling me that she was not pregnant after she had told us she was, was more than she could bear. She said that she and Nina talked about it and decided the best thing would be to simply move out of town! She and Chip and their three children would leave California rather than get on the phone and tell me that she really wasn't pregnant. But she was.

I called my mother. I had called Sue. I called everybody. We were pregnant!

For the first trimester, I was Sandra's worst nightmare. I was afraid of everything. I knew that she didn't smoke or drink. I knew that she took very good care of herself even when she wasn't carrying a child. But Sandra was so carefree about things, so not nervous. She was so relaxed in the world. I seemed perfectly willing to be anxious and agitated enough for both of us. I actually got on the phone with her and said, "Do you have an electric blanket? I heard that an electric blanket is not safe for the fetus. Are you using an electric blanket?" She had to live with this. Poor Sandra had to live with me for that first trimester. Sandra remained relaxed and carefree while I watched her under a telescopic lens. Every move she made. Every bite of food she took. I made sure she was drinking a glass of milk every day. I didn't want to be an annoyance and I certainly had no right to dictate what she was doing with her body, but I couldn't help myself! "Are you taking your prenatal vitamins?" She said, "No, I haven't gotten to the store yet, but I'll get them." I said, "Well, we're two weeks into this... aren't you supposed to take them from the very first day you know you're pregnant?" She said, "Yes, Yes. It's okay. I'm fine. Believe me. I'll go and get them." Then I had to call and annoy the doctor with this. "George, it's two weeks into Sandra's pregnancy and she hasn't started the prenatal vitamins." He said, "Yes?" Like he's waiting for me to say something of concern. "But shouldn't she be taking them?" He said, "She'll take them. She'll get them.

In a week or two she'll start taking them and she'll be fine." Can you imagine? I was a hovering, nauseous presence in Sandra's life. I was a hovering, nauseous presence in my own life! A lot of eye-rolling. Sandra did a lot of eye-rolling.

I would sometimes call her on the phone, and I could feel her eyes rolling through the receiver. Mostly her eyes rolled over my anxiety. I was scared that she would change her mind. I was scared that her children would talk her out of it. I was scared that the church would talk her out of it. I was scared that her mother-in-law would talk her out of it. I was scared of everything and everyone. But Sandra knew exactly what she was doing and why she was doing it and she knew there was no way anything tragic was going to happen. She simply had to endure my hyper-anxiety and fear. Sadly, I had achieved a position in life where I was something to be endured! Eye-rolling, a lot of eye-rolling.

The first trimester was the longest three months of my life. It felt like a year. At least a year. I had to restrain myself from calling Sandra every day, but if we didn't talk on the phone, I was sitting by the phone. I watched the phone, I watched the clock, I watched Sandra. I couldn't sleep. I never wasn't thinking about it. Miscarriage was the biggest fear. That's what happens when you get pregnant, isn't it? That's all that we knew. Every time the phone rang, I was scared. When Sandra called, she tried to talk to me like I was a normal person, but quickly came to realize it was not a normal person she was dealing with. She had to reconstruct how she spoke to me. The first thing she'd have to say when she called is "everything is fine." Then we could go on to find out why it was that she had called. The first trimester came and went, but it was a long three months for Sandra and an even longer three months for me.

SANDRA

Sandra was healthy, the fetus was healthy, I was sick. Sandra kept trying to tell me, "Karen, this is great. We're having a baby. This is a fun thing. This is a good thing." But my job was to be black. And I was as black as can be. I was the archangel of blackness. But every day that passed without a heartbreak brought us closer and closer to the birth. We also shared a lot of laughs and many loving and happy moments as well.

I met Sandra at every doctor's appointment. During the first trimester, you couldn't even see that she was pregnant. She was so slim and so lovely. I think she weighed about 110 pounds and is 5'6". But as we moved into the second trimester, for the first time, I began to see a little pouch protruding on her stomach and her pregnancy began to be visible. Every time I saw her, she looked more and more radiant. It was a staggering thing to behold. She was just so gorgeous. And she became more so the further along she got into her pregnancy. I don't mean she was gorgeous in the particular way a model was, but Sandra was beautiful. She was so wholesome and bright and she shined from within. And she was fit and healthy and strong.

It was at a doctor visit during the second trimester when we did the first sonogram. You can actually see the tiny fetus inside the womb. We were all there — Jim and Chip and Sandra and me. I have to admit that even I felt joy that day. The doctor put a gel on Sandra's stomach and used an apparatus which he rubbed back and forth on her stomach. On the monitor, we could see the inside of her uterus. At first, I couldn't see anything. It just looked like moving, squishy lines. And then the doctor pointed and said, "Look, there it is." And I looked over into the screen and I couldn't quite see, and he said again, "There, there." And Jesus God, all of a sudden, I could see a head and I could see a spine and I could see a foot. That was it; I was gone. I started to shudder with tears. It was more than I could contain. That there was a baby in there; our baby. The doctor stopped the camera and took pictures. The sex was still undetectable at this point. Then the doctor did something even more amazing.

He put a stethoscope on Sandra's stomach, and we were able to hear the heartbeat.

All of a sudden, out of the stillness, you could hear, "tadum, tadum, tadum, tadum." I lost it, I put my head on Sandra's shoulder, started to cry. She squeezed my hand and we both looked at the picture together and she said, "I told you. I told you." Joy. I felt joy.

Jim and I went home that day and for the first time, I think I actually began to believe that we were going to have a baby. Then we got a phone call. It was late in the evening. It was Sandra. She said, "We need to tell you guys something and we don't want you to worry." I moved right back to my address on Black Street. Then she said, "We are leaving Los Angeles. We're going to move. But there's nothing for you to worry about. Chip has been transferred to Sacramento. But I'll come back to Los Angeles for every doctor's appointment. Don't worry." I didn't like it. Did not like this at all. Talk about a feeling of no control. Sandra was taking herself and my baby out of town — across borders to another place, far away and there wasn't a thing I could do about it. Nothing. She said, "Karen, don't worry. I know you're sick. You're probably getting a feeling of concern, but there's nothing for you to worry about." And I said, "But what about Dr. Weinberger?" She said, "I'm going to come into town for the doctor visits.' I said, "That's a six-hour drive." She said, "Yes?" as if to say what's the problem?

I knew she was saying she would do it, but I couldn't believe that she could or should be expected to do that. And that meant another doctor and that meant opening the door to all kinds of problems. Again. I was sick. There are very few doctors who will work with surrogates. I was terrified that Sandra wouldn't be able to find a doctor or worse, would find one who would talk her out it.

I think we had one more doctor's visit here in Los Angeles and then they left.

We got a call. It was at night. Night-time calls were never good. Nobody calls at night with anything good to say. It was Sandra calling from Sacramento. Jim picked up the phone. She said, "Jim, everything is alright." This was how she had to begin every conversation. "Jim, let me talk to Karen." I picked up the phone, "Sandra?" She said, "Karen, I wanted you to be the first to know. I was just eating a chocolate chip cookie and I felt your baby kick for the first time."

I can't tell you how moved I was. What a beautiful thing that was for her to have done. I loved that she wanted to tell me first and not Jim and I loved the way she said it, "your baby just kicked for the first time." That call from all the way up in Northern California was the most reassuring thing I could have heard.

Sandra did drive down to Los Angeles for her doctor's appointments. She and Chip made that trip several times during the last trimester. They got somebody to watch their children, drove for six hours, saw the doctor, and drove six hours back. Can you imagine this woman? Now when I saw her, she looked PREGNANT! She was wearing maternity clothes and she looked radiant. She looked happy and she was happy. I would arrive at the doctor's appointment, oh, a good hour before we were to be there so I could sit there and be sick and wait for her to come. It was imperative to sit there and imagine her dying how many times in a six- hour drive from Northern California? How many car accidents could I imagine they had been in? I couldn't help it. Six hours on the freeway with my baby. Eventually, the door opened, and Sandra would walk in looking more refreshed after a six-hour drive than I would look after a long trip to Hawaii. She looked beautiful. She looked healthy. She looked happy. Chip was there. He did a lot of eye-rolling at me too. I became hyper-talkative when we got together. I never really knew what to say. Think about it. It's an awkward situation. It was calculated and artificial, yet intensely personal and full of intimacy. It was a bond of love, yet it was unusual, paradoxical, complex, and simple. You don't really know each other the way you do other friends and yet she's carrying your child.

I still felt, amongst other things, a tremendous strain to sell myself; to ensure that she would like me; to ensure that I wouldn't say or do anything wrong. Even then, I never really knew if, in the end, she would keep the baby or not. But that was me. I never really had to do that; that was all in my head. Sandra was so solidly on board from the second she said she would do it until the very end.

Sandra was getting big. We were in the last trimester. The doctor did another sonogram. Now you could really see a baby. This time you could see a penis and we knew it was a boy. The doctor printed out the sonogram and on the bottom of the tape he wrote, "A Hopkins-Fisher/Fund Production" During the ninth month of pregnancy, Sandra had to see the doctor once a week. And do you know that once a week, she and Chip drove six hours down and would turn around and go back up North after the appointment. They would make a twelve-hour drive, once a week, during that last month for a thirty-minute doctor's appointment. Sandra would say, "After you have children, you'll understand why I don't mind at all getting into the car for twelve hours by myself." She said that she would stick with this doctor and she did. She never missed an appointment.

She had decided long before that she and Chip were going to take a vacation after the birth. She wanted to go after the first week in February. We had agreed that Sandra would have the baby at Cedars Sinai and George would deliver the baby. Because we lived in Los Angeles and they were in Sacramento, everybody wanted to avoid Sandra's going into labor up North because she'd never be able to get down in time. The doctor had calculated that she would have the baby close to the third or fourth week of February. George explained that he could perform an amnio two weeks prior to the due date. The amniotic fluid would show if there was a complete development of the baby's organs, in particular the lungs, which were the last things to develop. If the results showed that the lungs were fully developed, George would induce labor and that's what he recommended we do. He told Sandra that if she wanted to take her vacation the second week in February, she should come to Los Angeles, he would do the test, if the baby's lungs were developed he would induce labor and a few days later she and Chip could go on vacation. Sandra said, "That's great. I know I'll be ready to deliver." She was always so confident about everything. And they don't come any more determined or reliable. She said, "But we won't go on vacation a few days later, I want to leave the hospital that day. Here's what's going to happen. I'm going' to come down. George will do the test. The results will show that the baby's developed and ready for delivery. I'll give birth and hang around for as long as you and the doctors want me to. You guys will stay with the baby and sleep in my hospital room. Chip and I will split. That's what's going to happen."

I passed the "Nationwide Baby Store" every day of my life to and from work. During all those years of infertility, inseminations, and miscarriages, I would look at the cribs and baby strollers through the window, but couldn't bring myself to walk in. I had not allowed myself to buy anything for the baby during the entire pregnancy. Sue, Reva (another close friend) and I had long since stopped paying any attention to our work. We had other things on our mind. After all, we were going to have a baby! There was no time for working. One day, in about the fifth or sixth month of the pregnancy, we decided that instead of not working in the office maybe we would leave the office and have a baby outing. Sue and Reva knew that I hadn't bought anything for the baby yet and suggested that we go to the store. We pulled into the parking lot and I began hyperventilating. I felt (you know) sick. We walked into the store, but as soon as I started looking around, I had to leave. I couldn't stay. I thought I was going to pass out. I had to get out of the store. I was so scared that this wasn't going to work. The closer we got to the birth of the baby, the more my terror mounted. While joy and expectation and excitement also mounted, so did fear. I was so worried something would go wrong and the later into the pregnancy it got, the worse the devastation would be if it did. The feeling that we were just not going to be allowed to have a baby was palpable and loud in my ears. I could not allow myself to be in that store for fear that it would trigger the attention of this God, whose attention had strayed for a while, and something terrible would happen.

So, the week before Sandra came down, I was in a frenzy. I really had a lot to do.

If all went the way it was supposed to, we were going to have a baby the following week. I had to go out and get a crib and a rocking chair and a chest of drawers and a mobile. I found a beautiful mobile and I turned it on, and it started to play "Somewhere Over the Rainbow." There was something about that song that sent me reeling. I had a crying jag in the baby store. I was buying things I never thought I would be holding in my hands. I bought the mobile and a carload of other things and came home and set up the baby's room. I put one of the teddy bears that I had bought in the crib and another in the bassinet. I set the mobile up over the crib, turned it on and just stood in that room listening to the music and praying.

Now the problem was our dog, Sol, who I had to keep dragging out of the bassinet. I would go into the baby's room and see this big, huge, smelly, honking, furry thing in the bassinet: Sol. I'd drag him out, he'd get right back in.

The last week was the worst. We had gotten past all the dangerous parts and I couldn't help but realize that this was really happening. There was tremendous excitement. There was no working that week. I remember sitting with Reva at a restaurant for hours. We'd sit there not saying anything for the longest time. I couldn't eat. I couldn't work. I couldn't talk. I couldn't do anything. It was just a time to be endured. I just had to live through it until Sandra came down. And she did. Thank God.

She and Chip arrived in Los Angeles at about seven in the evening. I was very anxious to show them the baby's room. I wanted her to see what we had done for this baby that she had been carrying for nine months, who she could feel kicking and who was making milk in her breasts. I wanted her to see where he was going to live. I hadn't put away anything that I had bought. I took everything out of the boxes, but I didn't put them in drawers. I laid them out on the dining room table like a banquet for Sandra to see. I think she was very pleased. I know she was. Sandra's motivation was the satisfaction, the extreme satisfaction of knowing that we would be parents who would turn ourselves inside out for this child. This was important to her. Knowing this child would be loved and cared for so much. Knowing this child, dearly wanted, would be raised in such a loving home. Her belief was that every child should have this. This is what being a family and parenting is all about but tragically, this isn't always the case. It brought Sandra immense joy to know that this was going to be the case with us.

We planned to get up very early in the morning and go to the hospital for the amnio test. It was an unreal situation waiting to go in to have this baby. At about ten that night Sandra said she was going to get their bags which they had left in the car. They were going to sleep in our guest room, and we'd go to the hospital together in the morning. We said goodnight.

The next morning, I was up early. I was just getting ready to do my hair and make-up because if the baby was born, I knew we would take videos that we would watch for years and my hair had to be right! I saw Chip, but I didn't see Sandra. Chip came to Jim and me and said, "I don't want you to panic, but last night when Sandra went out to get the suitcase from the car, she slipped on the wet walkway and cracked the small of her back and she can't walk. She's in extreme pain and hasn't been able to walk all night." I went into the bedroom. Sandra was as white as a sheet and in excruciating pain. She could not walk. We called the hospital and they said to put her in an ambulance and bring her over immediately. I never asked her if she could feel the baby kicking or not. I wanted to ask but she was in such tremendous pain she could barely speak. We arrived at the hospital and they snagged Chip to fill out the paperwork. We pushed through into the emergency room. I was so upset and so scared that the baby was dead. I didn't know if the placenta had been shaken loose when she fell, and she had been lying there all night long. She hadn't said anything reassuring and she didn't look well. It had been well over twelve hours since the accident. I found the doctor and frantically blurted out, "Doctor, this is Sandra, my name is Karen, Sandra's our surrogate, that's my baby in there, she fell down last night and she hasn't been able to walk or move in twelve hours." The doctor strapped a fetal monitor on her and wheeled her into the emergency room. I sat in a chair and waited. Within five minutes the doctor came out and took my hand.

"Your baby is fine. And Sandra is fine. But Sandra has started dilating so you're <u>going to have a baby</u>. We're going to take you up to maternity."

No amnio test. Sandra's accident started the birthing process and made an amnio irrelevant. She was having a baby! We went up to maternity. I was looking around and thinking, "My God, we're here. We're in the maternity room." The maternity ward at Cedar's is the most beautiful place on earth; at least I thought so at that moment.

When Sandra started dilating, the doctors gave her an epidural right away for the pain. Sandra said, "Whoa! That's great. What's that?!" The nurse said, "It's an epidural." Sandra said, "I never had that with my other three pregnancies." And I remember the nurse saying, "Honey, you're in Beverly Hills now!"

I never did wash my hair or put on my make-up. I was just getting ready to do that when Chip came in with the big news that Sandra was paralyzed, and my baby was dead! So, my hair was flat and I had no make-up on and that was all there was going to be to it. In these pictures that we would live with for an eternity, I would have flat hair and no make-up and that was just the way it was going to be. Sandra, however, did look beautiful. Somehow, her hair was brushed and she did have make-up on. Sandra has long, beautiful nails. She was calm and relaxed and her hands showed it. She even had earrings on and she was sitting in bed and she looked lovely.

Sandra was now comfortable. It must have been about eleven in the morning. It looked like we might be there a while, so Chip and Jim and I went to the cafeteria to get something to eat. I couldn't eat, but the guys ate something. We were just entering the room when George said, "You almost missed it! She's ten centimeters dilated and she's going to give birth any minute." We had only been in the hospital for a matter of hours when the actual birth started to happen. It began much sooner than anybody thought. Of course, Sandra had told us all along that she'd go in, have the baby, and that would be that. She wasn't kidding.

Sandra went into heavy labor. I don't know what she was feeling, but it was a tremendous ordeal for her body to be going through. At some point she was breathing and it was hurting her and I could see she was hurting so I started breathing for her. I can't tell you how stupid I looked on the video panting, but I wanted to do something to help her and there was nothing I could do. So, I was breathing. Two or three pushes later and out came the head. I was standing where I could see it. George said, "Push one more time, Sandra, just one more time." And out came the shoulders and the legs and then he was out.

The doctor picked him up, looked at me, and said, "Would the mother like to come and cut the cord?" And I came over and I cut the cord. It was very symbolic and very significant for me that I released the baby. They took him and gave him to a scrub nurse who started to clean him off and they put a little blue hat on his head. I followed the scrub nurse and couldn't stop looking at this baby. I couldn't have been more tentative or shy. What an acutely self-conscious moment that was, and yet the desire to hold him was overwhelming. I didn't really feel like I had the right to ask, but I wanted him. I said, "Can I hold him?"

I don't think she heard me and continued to wash him. I said, "Can I hold him?" Again, she didn't hear me. I said once again, "Can I hold him?" George came over and took the baby and then handed him to me.

I had always fantasized, long before I met Jim, about the moment I would first hold my baby in my arms. My fantasy was that my husband and my baby and I would make a threesome. I would be holding our baby and he would be leaning into me and we would make a circle. When George put the baby in my arms, without realizing it, I went not to Jim but directly to Sandra. I put the baby on the bed between Sandra's face and mine and couldn't stop crying and saying her name. "Sandra. Sandra.

Sandra." She looked at him and she touched his head and she looked back at me. We did it. The two of us did it. I didn't even realize that it wasn't Jim I had gone to. The first person I went to was Sandra. I went to Jim right after that and the three of us did make that circle. We stayed like that for a long time. It was quite a moment.

The final shot on the video is Jim and I holding the baby against the window in the background. Chip is holding Sandra's hand in the foreground. It's really something.

We named our son Benjamin David. Benjamin was then taken to this little area where they weigh him, and they put stuff in his eyes and put on a tiny diaper. Then I fed him for the first time. They had to teach me how to feed the baby with a tiny, tiny bottle and that was the beginning of realizing that these things don't come naturally. You have to learn how to do this. They taught me and I gave him his first bottle.

It was about seven or eight in the evening. Sandra said she was ready to go. She felt fine and she was ready to go on her vacation. The doctor examined her and said, "You can go." Everything happened exactly the way Sandra had predicted. We took her room and spent that night at the hospital with the baby. They went to our house to sleep. Jim and I lay on the bed all night watching this tiny infant through the plexiglass carrier and listened to him making squeaking noises. We called him "squeaky" for the first couple of days. We watched this baby in amazement and we knew everything was going to be all right.

I spoke to Sandra, who was still at our house, on the phone early the next morning and asked her how she was. She said she was fine. I said, "Where am I going to find the words,

Sandra, to say thank you to you?" I had said so many things to her throughout the nine months, a million things in a million different ways, but this was going to be the last time that I talked to her for a while. We didn't know what the future would hold for us. I knew that I would never let her leave my life, nor did I want her out of my life, but we didn't know exactly what form the relationship would take. "How do I find the words?"

She said, "Don't I know."

I said, "The doctor said that we could take the baby home."

She said, "You come home. We're leaving. Come on home."

They put me in a wheelchair and laid Benjamin in my arms and we were wheeled out of the hospital. We put him in the car and drove home with our baby. We were ready to begin our life together as a family. We opened up the door and on the dining room table was a note from Sandra reading: "Welcome Home Family. Enjoy the rest of your lives. We love you. Sandra and Chip."

For those who might think of surrogates as exploited and immensely sorry about their decisions when it's too late, let me tell you one more thing. The following year, Sandra called me on Mother's Day (a day of celebration I had wanted to enjoy for almost ten years.) She told me that being a surrogate mother was one of the most significant, defining, and happiest experiences of her life. It was something about which she felt extremely proud. She had done a lot of thinking, had talked to Chip and her children at great length, and wanted me to know that if Jim and I would like a sibling for Benjamin, she would do it one more time for us.

On August 16, 1993, our beloved daughter, Chloe Bess, was born.

SURROGATE

Karen L. Fund In Context

by David James Fisher

Karen L. Fund (1947–2012), the youngest daughter of Letty and Paul Fund, was born in Riverdale, New York in 1947. She mostly grew up in Englewood, New Jersey. Her sister Teddy (Thea Westreich Wagner) was born five years earlier during World War II. The Funds were an attractive and stylish couple. Paul worked as a venture capitalist, possessed leading man good looks, accompanied by a virile, athletic manner. He had played football in college, including a Rose Bowl appearance for the University of Alabama. He served in the Marines during the Second World War. Paul could be tough and insensitive in demeanor; Karen and I regarded him as having a strong paranoid streak to his personality. Letty was a tall, well dressed, and stylish woman with an artistic flavor, working as an interior designer. As a couple, the Funds were symbiotic, having little space for their baby girl Karen. They neglected and marginalized Karen, who was an anxious and insecurely attached infant, very eager for recognition, approval, and acceptance, which they rarely provided. For Karen, her parents were cold, narcissistic, critical, and intolerant. She always felt like an unwanted child and outsider. Her sister Teddy formed part of this union with Paul and Letty; she was not a particularly nurturing sibling, despite Karen's apparent vulnerabilities. It would take Teddy decades — and psychoanalytic treatment — to separate and individuate from her parents.

Karen was not an accomplished student, despite her high intelligence and creative inclinations, suffering from undiagnosed dyslexia and some learning difficulties. She did poorly at school. She found it time consuming and anxiety provoking, ultimately self-defeating, to read and absorb knowledge through books. To compensate, she became an adept listener and speaker, able to transmit information from the give and take of verbal exchanges. She was an excellent performer and developed a musical ear and receptivity to 1960's rock music.

Karen identified with and felt validated by the alienation and rebelliousness of rock in roll, by the poetic lyrics and raucous sounds of early Bob Dylan, the melodies and consolations of soft rock, the soulfulness and sadness of R & B, and above all the mournfulness and poignancy of Simon and Garfunkel, Van Morrison, and Crosby, Stills, Nash, and Young. She found the music of the Beatles inspiring, both life-affirming and witty, much preferring them to the Rolling Stones. Early in her adolescence, she learned to play bass guitar, joining a local rock group called the Jagged Edge. Karen herself had some jagged edges back then. She dressed in a way that blended masculine and feminine. She wore her long, dark, straight hair in a distinct 60's manner, while dressing in tuxedo pants and white shirt. Her photos show a beautiful and radiant face, slightly melancholic, resembling a cross between Liza Minelli and Karen Carpenter.

Karen's politics in the mid and late 1960's blended a radical from of opposition to the War in Viet Nam with a visceral resistance to racism and overt forms of bigotry. She was uninterested in theory, or in abstract discussions of injustice. She was the only white girl who went to Englewood's Dwight Morrow High School junior prom with a black boyfriend, very much against the wishes of her parents and to the astonishment of her classmates. Karen had to meet this young man, Benny Howard, in secret, sneaking into the prom together. Benny would subsequently become a jazz musician.

Karen practiced the politics of frontal confrontation rather than the ivory tower posturing of endless commentary and critical analysis. She participated in demonstrations at Columbia University, confronted Lyndon Johnson on Park Avenue in front of the Waldorf Astoria, marched in Washington D.C. against the War, was arrested at the Nixon White House after entering its grounds and diving into the swimming pool, wearing an American flag as a top. Hers were the politics of the hippies, mixing rock lyrics, libertarianism, an intuitive sense of right and wrong, and a fundamental distaste for parental, governmental, military, and academic authority. Karen was anti-authoritarian to the core. She also possessed a gut repugnance for middle class values and respectability, which she found hypocritical and life-denying. Karen was self-aware enough to realize that some of her rebellion sprang from a rejection of her parent's mentality and lifestyle; she had benefitted from some psychotherapy. This consciousness, combined with youthful vitality and vague utopian leanings, linked her to millions of individuals in her generation who opposed oppressive American policies domestically and abroad, the arrogance of power, and stultifying suburban outlooks. At other times, she suffered from massive anxiety and depression, stemming from isolation from her family and estrangement from establishment norms. Her existential dilemma turned on being an outsider while paradoxically wanting to be an insider. Karen was never entirely comfortable in either situation.

Emerging out of the anti-war movement and her commitment to civil rights sprang a commitment to the first wave of 1970's feminism. She gravitated to the feminist movement because much of its doctrine resonated, making her feel less alone, less invisible, less without a voice, in short, less subjugated as a woman. Karen experienced the domination of men and submission of woman not from reading Simone de Beauvoir, but from her lived experience of growing up in her family in middle class suburban America. She participated in early feminist meetings and marches, developing an identification with Gloria Steinem and Bella Abzug. She voiced solidarity with the feminists in the streets; gradually, feminist rhetoric saturated her everyday speech. Opposition to sexism encouraged her to read some feminist literature and journalism. She imbibed the substance and courageous spirit of 1970's feminism. She associated women with an oppressed majority, attempting to raise consciousness about their plight and to take measures fighting misogyny. No man could mess with her regarding these principles. And women who failed to recognize the explicit sexism and implicit injustices facing women made her sad and at times angry. She railed against this form of false consciousness, but would never have used that term.

And by the time we met in the summer of 1977, she was a passionate and highly articulate spokesperson for the economic and psychological equality of women. Over time, her anger would mellow and she became a mature voice and embodiment of the liberated woman's point of view. The first time I encountered her, she spoke eloquently about how women needed money, power, and position in the marketplace. In addition, Karen insisted that they required a safe space for personal growth, creativity, and self-expression. From this period of her life until her death, Karen functioned as a serious, proud, militant, card carrying feminist. Her feminist practices caused difficulties for some of her male bosses, who did not always embrace her essential concerns, and who questioned whether a radical feminist position was good for business. When she rose in the hierarchy into an authority figure, she only hired women, serving as a mentor, guide, and nurturing figure to the younger women who looked up to her.

As a teen-ager, Karen joined a rock band called the Jagged Edge, playing bass guitar. The band began to make a name appearing at the Night Owl Café (now Caffé Reggio) on McDougal Street in Greenwich Village — then the center of the music scene. Greenwich Village in that era was everything the suburbs and deluxe hotels (where her parents lived) were not. They opened for John Sebastian's folk rock group, The Lovin' Spoonful. On many nights, the audience pleaded for Karen to sing, shouting "let the chick sing." But unfortunately, Karen had no voice and could not carry a tune.

One night, Donovan's manager, Gypsy Dave, heard them perform, asking them to record several tracts. Donovan was himself a gifted folk-rock artist, considered by some to be the Bob Dylan of Great Britain. Karen and the Jagged Edge accompanied him on his tour of Los Angeles in the summer of 1966, playing live at the Whiskey a Go Go! on Sunset Boulevard, climaxing with a concert before twenty thousand fans at the Hollywood Bowl. Both the concert and the release of the record were enormous hits. "Sunshine Superman" became a number one hit single and "Season of the Witch" was widely acclaimed. Asked if they preferred one point on the album or a payment of nine hundred dollars, the band opted for the cash. Karen's gigs with Donovan were about the music and the thrill of playing on stage, not about the money. She was nineteen years old.

Karen's musical career came to an abrupt end in the late 1960's. Like many members of the counterculture generation, she had been living a life of excess, of living on the margins of society, a life, in effect, of recklessness, revolt, of dangerous drugs, and a hippie style of self-affirmation and self-destructiveness. In giving up these excesses and exiting from the music world, Karen entered a new phase of her professional life, that of a career in print media. As she emerged in the early 1970's, her career evolved in the direction of generating innovative ideas and brilliant concepts blending the realms of lifestyle, fashion, and popular culture. It was also a period in her life where she began to overcome her personal deficits and self-doubts.

In November, 1973, Karen became one of the founders, both editor and publisher, of *Millimeter*, a trade magazine for film and video. It is still being published. She worked as a publisher at the *Tucson Weekly* from 1978 to 1980, an alternative newspaper. She joined the *L.A. Weekly* first as a sales representative in Westwood, soon promoted to associate publisher. She was promoted because she generated lots of revenue for the free newspaper and because she was well respected and well liked. Karen was a gifted salesperson. The *Weekly* was an alternative, left-wing, counter-cultural newspaper, which positioned itself against the *Los Angeles Times*. Karen transformed it into a highly profitable, winning venture. She was responsible for selling advertising space in its pages and for leading a staff of mostly female sales representatives. She turned *The Weekly* into a cash cow by the middle 1980's, respecting the separation of church and state, of keeping editorial content distinct from advertising, and overcoming a myriad of obstacles internally within the newspaper and externally with the city of Los Angeles. It was a significant challenge to sell advertising for a radical, New Age, and provocative newspaper in the age of Reagan and Bush.

As an exceptionally competent salesperson, Karen was particularly strong at closing a deal. One of her earliest accounts at the *L.A. Weekly* was the discount department store, Adrays. Karen faced tough, male adversaries. They conducted the tense transaction about advertising one on one, two on one, often three on one, sometimes speaking English and sometimes Farsi. These tactics were designed to intimidate her. Karen and the owners of Adrays were close to an agreement after a prolonged negotiation. When they offered an insultingly low-ball proposal, reversing an earlier agreed upon number, Karen said, "I spit on your offer." Unable to push her around, realizing her formidable strength, the owners respected her as person. A full schedule of ads came in. Adrays became a steady and important source of revenue for the *L.A. Weekly*. Karen was determined, perseverant, and undeterred by obstacles or rejection. These qualities became operative in our own courtship and our pursuit of surrogacy adoption.

From 1985 to 1992, Karen served as co-founder and publisher of *L.A. Style*, a lifestyle and fashion monthly magazine. It was initially funded by the *L.A. Weekly* and for the first several years of its existence, she served as director of advertising sales for both publications. The *L.A. Style* phase of her career marked the highpoint of her success in print media. It was the fastest growing regional magazine in America; it had the highest growth of advertising revenue; it functioned as an antidote to the dull and predictable *Los Angeles Magazine*, which was threatened by its existence, by its oversize format, its award winning photography, its position at the cutting edge of cosmopolitan, post-Olympics Los Angeles. During Karen's tenure as publisher, *L.A. Style* had significant and growing revenues for a start-up magazine; she supervised and motivated a staff of sales representatives in Los Angeles, New York City, and Europe. When *L.A. Style* was purchased by American Express Publishing in 1988, Karen was retained as publisher, becoming a Vice President of American Express.

As publisher, she functioned as a dynamic feminist manager, leading her staff with strength, optimism, and a soft-spoken voice. She affirmed her co-workers, cultivated their talents, took pride in their successes, and was kind about their weaknesses and limitations. Karen inspired others through an exceptional ability to form and sustain relationships, to understand the needs and aspirations of her clients, and a formidable ability to close a deal. This period of time coincided with a painful and persistent infertility crisis and with our attempts to explore surrogate adoption. It was a paradoxical moment of her life, one of high fulfillment and achievement, but also of feelings of uncertainty, failure, and anxiety about whether she would ever be a mother, or that we would have a family.

There was a morning in New York City when Karen represented *L.A. Style* in the late 1980's. She first met with Michel Roux, who directed the advertising for Absolute Vodka and then with Leonard Lauder, CEO of Estee Lauder. They were high-powered and entitled clients, accustomed to deference from magazine publishers, and used to getting their way. Karen sold over fifty pages of four-color ads that morning, taking in over a half million dollars in revenue, an enormous success for one morning.

At the height of her professional life in the early 1990's, Karen was interviewed by Richard Schlossberg, publisher and CEO of the *Los Angeles Times*. Schlossberg asked Karen about the size of *L.A. Style's* cash flow. She confidently said that it was fourteen million dollars a year. He said those numbers were "peanut shit." For us, the number was extraordinary, a real source of accomplishment. Then, he asked if she would consider taking over responsibility for revenue for the *L.A. Times* daily, which was billing out one billion dollars a year. Originally, Karen believed she was being interviewed for the Sunday Magazine section of the *Los Angeles Times*.

Karen, it must be noted, had no particular desire to affiliate or collaborate with *The Times*. Coming from the counterculture, yet imbued with an entrepreneurial spirit, equipped with an astute understanding of other people and herself, she knew she was ill-suited for corporate America and for the corporate culture of *The Times*. The peanut shit interview, as she dubbed it, showed Karen's excellent judgment about what was a good fit for her, where she might feel recognized, creative, relatively at home, and free to pursue her own version of a print media career. There would be other job possibilities in these years, including offers from American Express Publishing to take on the responsibilities of being a publisher of a national magazine. Karen refused these offers, knowing full well she did not wish to move to New York, knowing that my psychoanalytic practice was in Los Angeles, and realizing that L.A. was our home base. By 1985, both of us were making money, especially Karen, and we had purchased our first home in the Beverly-Fairfax section of Los Angeles.

Karen's brilliance as a negotiator was also demonstrated in 1992-93, one year after Benjamin's birth. At the time, she functioned as Chairperson of the Board at the *L.A. Weekly*. With consummate skill and tact, she succeeded in brokering a deal that sold the *L.A. Weekly* to the *Village Voice*, an important alternative newspaper in New York City. The sale involved deal making and negotiating at the most subtle levels. Not only was the *L.A. Weekly's* Board severely divided, after years of accumulated personal rivalries, feelings of betrayal, and political rancor, but also dealing with the *Village Voice's* due diligence were daunting responsibilities. Once again, Karen proved herself to be a champion closer, able to mediate conflicting groups and personalities, and focused on achieving a desire goal — in this case the sale of *The L.A. Weekly*.

During the middle 1980's Karen underwent a rapid transition away from being a high-powered print media specialist toward motherhood. She desired to be a mother. As her book *Surrogate* documents, this wish to be a mother and to start a family became increasingly urgent, persistent, and increasingly frustrating. Karen and I experienced a long infertility crisis, one that lasted many years. We experienced it very differently. And though it is impossible to measure such life events, she took it much harder than I did. As a man, I was struck by the irony of having my earliest years of life spent not wanting to get a woman pregnant. Now when I wished to impregnate my wife, we were unable to conceive. We tried over and over again.

Karen cried and got dejected when she got her period. Her hopes were raised and brutally dashed every month. We consulted with the leading medical and gynecological specialists of the day. We had intercourse during her days of ovulation, our love life interrupted by the persistent pressure of our desire to get pregnant, distorted by the presence of the thermometer. This injured our previously satisfactory sexual relationship, robbing it of spontaneity, romance, and passion. Our sex life became controlled by the necessity to fertilize and by the exigencies of the time of the month.

Karen, for her part, had strong emotional reactions to friends and family who began their families. Stoked by her intense longings to be a mother, she was envious and resentful of the successes of other women. She disliked herself for her envy, becoming self-blaming. She felt helpless, incompetent, and incomplete as a woman — thinking of herself as a failure. Perhaps Karen's intense desire to become a mother contained something reparative in her own development. Being a mother might help her to overcome the lasting legacy of having had a bad-enough mother, of having deficient parenting.

Karen's experience of a long crisis of infertility beautifully chronicled in *Surrogate* gave rise to a sense of powerlessness and futility at not being able to conceive. Coexisting with her anxiety about the situation was an underlying depression, epitomized by feelings of sadness, despair, and mourning over the lost possibilities of pregnancy. Most seriously, she experienced a regressive helplessness. Karen struggled mightily against the infantilizing feelings and associations with infertility. She often spoke of her sense of incompleteness and emptiness. She entered into therapy with a female analyst, discussing her grief at not being able to bear a child. It is quite possible, but never articulated consciously, that Karen's inability to get pregnant may have been linked to an unconscious phantasy that I might leave her, possibly for a younger and more fertile partner. She always suffered from severe abandonment anxiety, after having been traumatized by neglect, distance, and rejection by her parents and sister. I am speculating about this dynamic. During the entire project of researching and implementing surrogacy, we functioned as partners and as a team. The desire to become parents was mutual, drawing us into a deeper intimacy, as were the shared disappointments and joys.

During the protracted infertility process, it was discovered that my sperm was motile and viable. Unfortunately, Karen suffered from scarred and obstructed fallopian tubes, the result of wearing an IUD, a Dalkon Shield for many years. The IUD caused an infection, which then resulted in extensive damage to her fallopian tubes. The Dalkon Corporation, manufacturer of the Dalkon Shield, was sued by many of its users, who were awarded millions of dollars in compensatory and punitive damages. Karen never sued. To reverse the pelvic inflammatory damage to her fallopian tubes, Karen underwent laparoscopic surgery at Cedars-Sinai Hospital. The surgery failed. Several months after the procedure, the scarring returned.

We had agreed that Karen's laparoscopic surgery would be the last invasive procedure we would use in order to facilitate natural pregnancy. We began to explore other options of parenthood. For some complex reasons, some rational, and some irrational, I desired to have a biological linkage to my child. Clearly, there was a piece of narcissism in this choice. I realized then that I would have gotten attached to an adopted child, but I still wished for a genetic tie. In an act of generosity, Karen agreed to my wish and we began to investigate the possibilities of a surrogate adoption. Surrogacy was entirely a new reproductive technology in the later 1980's and we were uncertain about our options. After so many episodes of perceived failure on her part, Karen questioned whether parenthood would ever happen for us, being skeptical that we would come through the process as parents with a baby in our arms.

Some of the most riveting passages in *Surrogate* speak to Karen's worries about moving forward with surrogate adoption. At the time there were no federal or California laws regulating surrogacy, hence very few adequate guidelines or precedents. Many of my psychoanalytic colleagues were unhelpful about us entering into the process, uttering critical and judgmental remarks about us pursuing a surrogate path forward to parenthood. It was as if surrogacy subverted a sacred law of motherhood, violating the current dominant theory about the deep attachment of the infant and child with the biological mother. In privileging psychologically the conventional course of conception, including adoption, the analytic community seemed to us morally opposed to surrogacy; at times various outspoken members of the community indicated that they believed surrogate adoption was inappropriate — a term veiling their own insensitivity to our plight and to our desires to begin a family, a term disguising their punitive form of judgment.

The one exception to the pervasive pattern of moralizing and of implicit opposition to surrogacy came out of several important conversations with my friend Bruno Bettelheim, then living in Los Angeles. Despite his age and compromised medical condition, despite his depression, Bettelheim lucidly and forcefully urged Karen and me to move forward on the surrogacy path. The author of *A Good-Enough Parent* thought we would fulfill the task outlined in his book, assessing that we were sufficiently mature and grounded to provide a safe, trusting, and playful home for a child. He was rather fond of Karen, thinking of her as competent and high-powered as a businesswoman (Somewhat idiosyncratically, he was impressed that she had a car phone, which was an uncommon thing in the late 1980's). Bettelheim counseled us to seek out legal consultation to protect us if the surrogate changed her mind, wanting to keep the baby. Some of his concern, consistent with our own anxiety about the matter, had to do with the highly publicized case of Mary Beth Whitehead, who did change her mind and sued the adopting parents for custody of the child after birth. Bettelheim also asked his son Eric, an attorney, to inquire about protection we might have if the surrogate mother changed her mind. We learned through his son and our own researches that there were no legal precedents. California had no laws regulating surrogacy. This was a new, innovative, and untested reproductive technology. We were among the pioneers in pursuing this option and we increasingly understood the risks. But the rewards greatly outweighed them.

There was one other significant moment concerning Bettelheim in our surrogacy adventure. I had left a somber message on his voice mail that our first surrogate, Llana Lloyd, had developed a tubal pregnancy, requiring us to abort the pregnancy. After several weeks of elation, our joy turned to dejection, almost to despair. I can still remember the anguish and grief that Bettelheim conveyed in his consolation message to me, saying how sad he was for us that we were experiencing this loss. I will always be moved — and educated — by his attunement in that bleak hour. Empathy was transmitted in the tone of his message, his genuine affect, rather than in the words or his capacity to imagine our shock and disappointment. He would subsequently support us to continue the surrogate journey.

When Karen and I seriously decided to commit to surrogacy adoption, Karen was very troubled by the Mary Beth Whitehead case and by an unnuanced anti-surrogacy campaign led by leading American feminists, including Gloria Steinem, Betty Friedan, Phillis Chesler, and Marilyn Friend. While she and I expected the Catholic Church and fundamentalist Christian groups to be opposed to surrogacy, Karen was disturbed by the simplistic and rhetorically violent polemic led by leading feminist voices against her decision to pursue beginning our family. As a committed feminist, she now felt turned upon by her feminist sisters.

Mary Beth Whitehead served as a surrogate for William and Elizabeth Stern. Baby M. was born in March, 1986. Whitehead then announced that she wanted to keep the baby. A court case ensued. The Sterns were awarded full custody. This was the first American court verdict on surrogacy; we were aware and wary that few safeguards and guidelines existed for surrogacy. Karen's desire to be a mother was now being denounced as a step in the "commercialization of reproductive technologies." Upset and temporarily put on the defensive by the economic argument that surrogacy exploited poor women, accused of being part of an "elite economic class" using a poorer group as breeders, Karen felt abandoned by her feminist cohort, radically misrecognized, with her intentions misrepresented. Friedan summed it up by stating that the present policy on surrogacy "dehumanizes, depersonalizes, and commodifies women." The Baby M. case, with its national publicity and mostly anti-surrogacy backlash, reinforced Karen's anxiety that Sandra might change her mind and keep the baby. It also made her feel more isolated and misunderstood in her community of empowered and articulate women. It was sad to her that leading feminists had so little empathy for working women who desired to be mothers. We subsequently learned, paradoxically, that Sandra worried that we might change our minds and not accept the child she was carrying for us. At no point in the surrogacy process did Sandra or Chip ever indicate that money was a prime motivator in their decision. Having twice agreed to do it, they never expressed any sense of being dehumanized, or that they were complicit in baby selling.

Our first-born Benjamin D. Fisher was born on February 7, 1991; Chloe B. Fisher followed on August 16, 1993. When Karen left her professional life to become a full-time mother, she brought the same level of intensity to the work and challenges of being a mom. Until she became sick, she did all the mundane and significant things that mothers do: carpooling, teacher conferences, arranging play dates, participating in their lives as a caring and nurturing guide. She was present at the kids' athletic and school events, being supportive and attentive to their anxieties and aspirations. She was particularly brilliant at the Admissions' interview at the Center for Early Education, where both children attended. She transmitted to the children her sense of compassion, sympathy for the underdog, smart and informed decision making, and learning how to relate to others in a sensitive and not self-centered way. She passed on to them her opposition to racism and gender discrimination. She conveyed her love for them in times of trouble and crisis, her devotion at moments of success and important rites of passage. Though she would have liked to live to see them reach adulthood, Karen provided a solid foundation for them to grow, be self-aware, and function as responsible citizens and members of the community.

Karen was diagnosed with Hepatitis C in late 1999. To attempt to cure or slow down the progression of the disease, she underwent three lengthy, arduous series of treatments, consisting of a cocktail of chemotherapy injections of interferon and ribavirin. For her, the treatment was worse than the disease. She suffered from the side effects of the chemotherapy with flu like symptoms, fatigue, loss of hair, moderate to extreme depression, confusion, and short-term memory loss. To make matters even more dire, she developed several auto-immune diseases in the last four years of her life, including a severe case of neuropathy, diseases of her gums and teeth, problems with her gait and balance, and shooting pains in her feet and ankles. There were days when she was in agony. There were limits to the treatment of the auto-immune illnesses because of the pre-existing condition of hepatitis-C. During the last years of her life, Karen had seven doctors, all top specialists, all increasingly unable to help her to recover or survive. She lived these final years just as she had lived previously; she fought a valiant fight, maintaining her dignity and relatively good spirits in the face of destructive illnesses, a bodily and mental assault, that would have been shattering to anyone's sense of self. Karen was resilient to the end, even good-humored about a mortal struggle that was not in the least funny. If her doctors agreed on anything, it was a consensus on Karen's courage.

One of Karen's lasting legacies is her book *Surrogate*. In her own words and voice, she articulated her genuine and ferocious struggle to become a mother and to begin a family. Throughout the text, Karen is honest, self-deprecating, and at times very funny. In it, she also expresses her authentic gratitude to Sandra for giving her and us the greatest gift of all, the gift of life. Karen never expected to die so young, so see her quest for motherhood ruptured so abruptly. Though cut short by her illness and death, Karen's life had several distinct chapters: music, feminism, publishing, prominence in print media, marriage, and parenthood. It was a life well lived, full of challenges, diversity, and accomplishment. It was marked by love and care toward our children, toward friends, and co-workers. Karen lived and died with a generosity of spirit that was exceptional.

A Conversation with Sandra Hopkins

by David James Fisher

―――・―――

THROUGH STUPIDITY OF MY OWN, I was learning all about life's hard knocks. But the one thing I loved that came easy for me was being pregnant. We already had three beautiful children of our own and had made permanent plans not to have any more through my husband's vasectomy. I loved being a parent and felt sad for couples that wanted children, but were unable to experience that joy. I wanted to do something intentional with my life. So, I decided to become a surrogate. Since I loved being pregnant and did not want any more children of my own, it was an easy decision for me. I had not discussed this with my husband Chip, but I knew he would not care what I did as long as I was happy.

I thumbed through the yellow pages and found a psychologist named Nina Kellogg. I told her my intentions. She asked if I had a spouse and children of my own. She asked if I had discussed this with my husband. I told her no. She told me to talk to him, then if we were in agreement, she would invite us both to come and sit with her to discuss the whole process to determine whether or not I was a candidate. We met with Nina and I was super excited.

After a meeting with Nina, we had a two-week waiting period. I was so excited, and I was telling everyone I knew. The anticipation and joy that I was expecting was far from the negative response I received. Although most were excited for me, there were a few naysayers in the group. However, my determination overshadowed the doubters.

The day finally arrived that we got to meet Karen and Jim. I had told my husband when we arrived at Nina's office that if I felt uneasy in any way that I would drop it and never discuss it again. My heart melted as soon as I met Karen. I could see Jim beamed with excitement over the love for his wife. He was very tender and caring. You could tell he only wanted to have a family with the woman that he loved so much. That was evident.

As Karen unfolded her story with all of her physical and emotional pain, my heart broke. As the meeting ended that day, Karen hugged me and said, "even if you decide not to choose us, we are honored that you would take the time to come and meet us."

On the drive back to Lancaster, I told my husband Chip if he was okay with my going forward that it was my heart's desire to become a surrogate. He smiled and said he wanted me to be happy and he was behind me one hundred per cent. We then had a two-week waiting period. When the time was up, I called Nina and told her I was ready to begin. We met for some time and did some counseling which was a major healing of some old childhood wounds in my life. I am forever grateful to Nina for her expertise and care.

Nina at once called Karen. Karen would later show me a small piece of paper with the writing of the message from Nina to Karen that read, "Karen, I think I found your miracle."

A few months later we would receive the great news that Karen and Jim were expecting. As I begin to show, we made it clear to our three children that this was not our baby, but it belonged to Karen and Jim. Our son was once asked by his teacher when his baby brother or sister was arriving. He stated it's not our baby, it's Karen's and Jim's baby. The teacher was so stunned that she had to call me for verification. We are so proud of our kids.

I was happy to share everything about the pregnancy with Karen. Morning sickness, back pain, and insomnia are a few examples of what I related to her. But I remember being so excited one evening around eleven P.M., I called her. The first words out of my mouth were the baby is fine and your baby just kicked!!! She was laughing, crying, and screaming all at the same time. I am glad we got to share that moment. The day Benjamin finally arrived there was joy in Karen and Jim just like I expected. They were beautiful parents that now felt and seemed complete.

Less than two years later Karen called me one afternoon. As soon as I heard her voice, I asked her if it was time for a sibling. She laughed and said are you willing? I said of course I am. Not too much later they would be holding their baby girl Chloe. The once sad and empty parents now had their bundles of joy.

Karen and I unfortunately lost touch with each other several years down the line. My thought was that they were ready for their own family. I wanted to honor that, so I did not pursue trying to find them. Two years after Karen had died, I wondered about all of them in my heart. My heart hurt with not knowing, but I trusted Jesus was watching over them. Several years later I searched Karen's name on the Internet and up popped her obituary notice. My heart was broken. I cried and grieved as if I had just lost my best friend. Even though we have not seen each other for many years, we would always share a common bond.

I was thrilled when just three years ago Chloe contacted me. What an amazing young lady she is! She has a beautiful smile just like her mother, the same energy, and the genuine concern about me.

I am happy that this story is being told.

JIMMY: Why did you want to be a surrogate in the first place? Why did you suggest we do it a second time?

SANDRA: I wanted to be a surrogate because, number one, I loved being pregnant and didn't want any more babies. Chip and I were having a difficult time. When I was pregnant, I was a great wife, but I definitely didn't want more kids. Then I realized how much I loved being a parent and the thought that people could not have children broke my heart. I suggested it a second time because I wanted Ben to have a sibling. And I knew how much love you had to pour into one baby, and I knew a second one would be a breeze. And I was right.

JIMMY: How did your Christian faith figure into your decision?

SANDRA: It honestly didn't. At the time we were going to church. But I was not in a relationship with Jesus at that time. It was merely on paper — for — to everybody else how it looked good. So, I didn't even factor Christianity into that. But I loved God even during that time, even when I was being unfaithful to him.

JIMMY: Did you feel that you were doing God's work in doing this extraordinary thing?

SANDRA: Not even a little bit. I didn't even consider God, as bad as it sounds. But I was excited to be a surrogate and so, no, it did not play a role.

JIMMY: Was this gift a pure form of Christian love?

SANDRA: Again, I would have to say no.

JIMMY: Your marriage to Chip was in crisis around the time of being a surrogate. How did becoming a surrogate help you repair your relationship with Chip, how did it bring you closer together?

SANDRA: Well, it helped repair our relationship because it was during that time, Nina [the psychotherapist] helped me out tremendously. We believe in the supernatural because I've seen it over and over. This period was one of those times. God had moved us from Bakersfield to Madera, Madera to Lancaster. We got to Lancaster and I discovered the same friend who had been with me in Bakersfield and Madera had also moved to Lancaster near there, a few miles away. We became friends and she told me about how she had been sexually abused as a child and how it

	had affected her now. I was able to talk with Nina about that, bringing healing and closure to that deep wound in my life.
JIMMY:	This may be a painful issue, but were you sexually abused or molested as a child or adolescent?
SANDRA:	Yes, I was. I have talked about it before. I would like to share this with you, but right now I do not have the strength to discuss it.
JIMMY:	What was it about Karen that helped you to be sympathetic to her desire to be a mother and to bond with her? You seemed to have a very real affection for one another.
SANDRA:	Okay, this question makes me cry. There was a bond of real affection between us. She was so genuine, and you were too Jimmy, but it's different from woman to woman. She understood women and I was so sad that I did not get to have her in my life. I felt that we bonded like sister to sister right off the bat from the very first time that I met you guys. Yeah, I missed her. When I read her obituary, it just sickened me and saddened me. I cried. I know you guys miss her like crazy. I didn't know her that long, but she really blessed my life and we shared a beautiful family together.
JIMMY:	What was it about me that helped you decide to assist me to become a biological father?
SANDRA:	Jimmy, you're just so honest, so real, so matter of fact, like my husband. It was hard not to love you because you were her rock, her pillar, her

	encourager, and her cheerleader. Chip was the same to me and I saw those qualities in you. I thought this guy is going to make a wonderful father and you have. I haven't got to know Ben at all, but Chloe is just a beautiful girl, inside and out. The sad part of dying soon is not having gotten to know her and you a little more.
JIMMY:	Did the process of twice being a surrogate contribute to your growth and development as a woman and a human being? Was it maturational?
SANDRA:	It definitely matured me, no doubt about that. I think it did because it gave me a better understanding of who I was. I realized I had the ability of love that I could possess because of Christ dwelling in me. Because on my own I tried it and I clearly fell short for twenty-eight years. I loved being a surrogate. It helped me to grow up and to truly love.
JIMMY:	How important was therapy with Nina Kellogg?
SANDRA:	It was again a God situation. I never could have afforded counseling back then. I was naïve. It just didn't dawn on me the degree of knowledge you have with counseling — even Karen, she would have been a huge mentor/teacher for me. Having Nina to work through that whole molestation process was a total God-blessing.
JIMMY:	How important an event was this in your life as you reflect back on your years on this earth — is it something you are proud of?

SANDRA: Good question. Oh absolutely, I am proud. I was just thinking I sure wish I had Chip here because he had so much insight on different things. He even went to my counseling with me after he got sick in October 2018. He shed light with the counselor and talked again about some issues. I sure wish he was here to add more to this because he would have been so helpful. He was proud of me, I was proud of myself, proud that I had the opportunity, that I was blessed to do it. I feel like God put you guys right there in our lives. I know he did, and I am so thankful. I pray for you guys all the time that you will know that peace and joy because of Jesus one day.

JIMMY: Was it hurtful that you did not have contact with us after the kids entered school?

SANDRA: Yes, it did hurt, but I understood, not realizing Karen had been sick. I thought you two were wanting to separate. I thought, hey we're a family now, and I wanted to respect that. When my letter came back in the mail that you guys had moved, it seemed like the ending point. I was happy and I prayed that someday I would get to meet you guys. God honored that prayer. I told Chloe from the time she was in my womb and from the time before she was even conceived that I started praying that God would show you what an awesome God he is, what a wonderful plan he has for her life. So yeah, it was sad, but I totally understood that and wanted to honor it.

JIMMY: Karen and I are Jewish and not Christian, how did that factor into your decision, if at all?

SANDRA: It didn't. Jews are God's chosen people, so if anything, you're up there on the higher end than me, right?

JIMMY: Would you recommend the process to other sensitive, caring, and strong women?

SANDRA: Yes and no. It takes somebody very unique to do it. But it takes a very special and strong person that can be a surrogate because you get a lot of criticism. When I first decided that I wanted to be a surrogate, I was excited. I believed I could do this. I loved being pregnant and I thought this is going to be so great. I was excited and when I started hearing people going, "You're giving your child away?" And I'm like, "No, no, no, no, it's Karen and Jim's." Some said, "It's your egg." I went wow, I never looked at it that way. I'm not sure if this was my immaturity, just not realizing it. I don't know. But I've never regretted it. I am thrilled the children got to be loved by Karen for as long as they did and that they still have you. And I'm praying that someday, we'll bond with each other.

JIMMY: Were there any surprises in the process?

SANDRA: No, but I remember after we moved back to Lancaster after Madera, it was during that whole time as a surrogate, there was a scandal about surrogacy, maybe it was in New York. They wanted to keep the baby and I remember watching TV that morning going (gasp) "What if Karen and Jim decided they didn't want to keep the baby, oh my gosh I would have four kids – What would I do with four kids? What would I do with another baby, oh my gosh! I almost panicked and I called Karen that morning and I went, "Karen, you for sure want your baby, right?" And she says strongly, "Oh yes, Sandra, yes, I do." So that was kind of a comical surprise.

JIMMY: You said these babies were Karen and Jim's. What about ways in which a pregnant woman gets attached to the fetus, did you experience sadness or depression when you resumed your life and gave us our family?

SANDRA: I didn't. I don't know if you remember that I fell and hurt my tailbone [the night before Ben's birth]. The day of the delivery you guys stayed at the hospital and we left for San Diego. I was in agony for months with that … my coccyx. So, I didn't even have time to have post-partum blues like you can with pregnancy. I never had that with my kids, and I didn't this time. I was just so excited for you and I just wish I would be right there, a little fly on the wall, to watch all the kisses and hugs and love that those children got and are still receiving.

JIMMY: Was it awkward for you to have Karen and I in the birthing room while Chip was with you videoing the birth?

SANDRA: I would not have had it any other way. You guys had to be there. You know I am not a prideful woman in that aspect, so no, it didn't bother me. I was so excited. And that's why I wanted Karen to hold that baby, to be the first to hold him. Good memories, I should watch that video again … nah … I might not … it might hurt then I'd cry because I was hurting.

JIMMY: Did Chip feel the surrogate experience also changed his life in a positive or negative way?

SANDRA: Nothing negative at all about this whole entire process. Just a unique time of our life. Yes, we grew as a couple. It was a bonding time in our life, a brand-new start for us. It was a brand-new start for you. Even our kids, even Amanda and Chloe, are friends now. My kids welcome you guys with open arms any time you want.

JIMMY: Was money a motivating element in your choice to become a surrogate?

SANDRA: Money was NEVER EVER a factor. In fact, I didn't even know I was getting paid until Nina told me. In the end I am not sure how much money we actually got because driving down every week in our old clunker used lots of gas. I'm thankful your children have brought you so much joy.

A Surrogate Daughter's Ambivalence

by Chloe B. Fisher

For as long as I can remember I've known that I was a product of surrogacy. My dad would joke saying it was harder for his children to absorb that he'd been married once before he had met my mom than it was for us to understand that we were biologically conceived by another woman.

I always had an interest in meeting Sandra. I wondered if we resembled one another and I was curious about her ancestry. I fantasized about what Sandra looked like. I only had a few pictures while she was pregnant with me upon which to base those fantasies.

My curiosity in looking up Sandra intensified in high school. It also coincided with my mom's declining health. The more my mom's energy was spent battling her illness, the more I starved for a mother figure. I began looking Sandra up online, writing down telephone numbers. I must have called once, maybe twice, during one of my mom's frequent admissions to the hospital, but I was unable to get ahold of her. I knew my parents would support my search for Sandra, yet I kept quiet as my curiosity piqued. My mom's health was fragile and the last thing I wanted to do was to disrupt her state of psychological and physical vulnerability.

When I was sixteen years old, I delved further into the process of looking up Sandra. My mom and I had an emotional exchange. I picked her brain about Sandra's personality, not revealing that I had her telephone number in my room, and that potentially I might call her. My mom was giving me the typical spiel about Sandra's kind heart when I abruptly stated that I didn't need to meet her. I told her that I only had one mother and how loved I felt as her daughter. I explained that she was more than enough for me. I don't know what possessed me to make that assertion. In part, it was a lie; I did want to meet Sandra. On some level, I must have known it's what my mom needed to hear. I look back at the moment wondering if her tears were because she was touched, or if she needed that reassurance from me as she slipped further into her illness. Wanting to protect my mom as much as I could, I decided then I would put my search for Sandra on hold. I suspect that my mom might have felt threatened, possibly secondary, because she missed out on the experience of being my biological mother. Despite her not being my birth mother, I never wanted to validate the notion that I did not think of her as my real mom. My mom's tears confirmed that she was in no place for me to open up old wounds around infertility and inner conflicts about surrogacy.

About four years after my mom passed away, during the summer after I graduated from college, I finally worked up the courage to contact Sandra. After we connected, we immediately made plans for me to drive up to meet her and her big family. It was overwhelming emotionally, but they were nothing short of warm and inviting. Sandra and I spent the weekend getting to know one another and freely asking each other all types of questions. It was easy and mostly comfortable. Sandra and her family were devout church members who often referenced Jesus and quoted the bible. As a child of two secular New York Jews, hearing all the Christian bible talk made my head spin.

Despite how lovely Sandra was, I left her house that weekend ambivalent about wanting to maintain a relationship with her. We were biologically connected, sure, but on some level, I felt as if developing a friendship with Sandra would erase or override my mom's existence and fond memories of her. Rationally, I knew that wasn't the case. I also knew that was not Sandra's intention. Beyond that, I'm certain my mom would have supported our relationship. Nonetheless, I felt guilty, caught in a bind between loyalty to my mom who had brought me up and to my birth mother Sandra. I would struggle to find answers. A few months after we met, Sandra gave me the unfortunate news that she had stage four breast cancer.

After reading my mom's book *Surrogate*, I tried to reconcile how Sandra chose my mom and dad for the surrogacy. From my perspective now, and after knowing both of them, it's hard to imagine an intimate interaction between Sandra and my mom. They came from different cultural and social backgrounds with distinct personalities. I don't quite see them belonging together. I did not easily grasp their bond. I get it now. There's something about them, something very empathic, caring, and loving that springs from the depths of their inner beings. It's why I constantly hear past and present stories of people gravitating towards them. I have a recurring fantasy of having all three of us in a room together. While it pains me that my mom and Sandra will never get the opportunity to reunite, or that I'll never be able to experience all three of us together, I still feel that my mom's version of the story is both beautiful and moving. I am sometimes astonished it all worked out so well. Thinking of myself as the daughter of surrogacy, I most consistently feel gratitude. I feel lucky that destiny, or fate, converged to create me.

It's been eight years since I lost my mom and the pain still remains. Sometimes the grief about her loss is small enough for me to contain and process; and at other times, the sorrow engulfs me, the grief becomes unbearable. Above all, when I think about her soft voice and velvety skin, I feel so thankful that I got nineteen years with her. She was a kind and exceptional woman and truly outstanding as a mother.

Karen L. Fund biography

Karen L. Fund (1947-2012) was the Publisher and a founder of *L.A. Style*, a lifestyle and fashion magazine. She was also Associate Publisher of *The L.A. Weekly*, subsequently serving as Chairperson of its Board of Directors. After a career in rock music and advertising, she emerged as a major figure in print media in Los Angeles. Married to psychoanalyst David James Fisher for thirty-one years before her untimely death, Karen Fund was the loving and devoted mother of Ben Fisher and Chloe Fisher.

www.ingramcontent.com/pod-product-compliance
Lightning Source LLC
Chambersburg PA
CBHW072036110526
44592CB00012B/1441